TOP 10
BRUSSELS & BRUGES
ANTWERP & GHENT

D1407399

Left **Hôtel de Ville, Grand Place, Brussels** Right **Belgian truffles**

DK

LONDON, NEW YORK,
MELBOURNE, MUNICH AND DELHI
www.dk.com

Produced by DP Services,
31 Ceylon Road, London W14 0PY

Reproduced by Colourscan, Singapore
Printed and bound in China by
Leo Paper Group

First published in Great Britain in 2004
by Dorling Kindersley Limited
80 Strand, London WC2R 0RL
A Penguin Company
Reprinted with revisions in 2006, 2008, 2010

**Copyright 2004, 2010 ©
Dorling Kindersley Limited, London**

All rights reserved. No part of this
publication may be reproduced, stored in a
retrieval system, or transmitted in any form
or by any means, electronic, mechanical,
photocopying, recording or otherwise,
without the prior written permission of the
copyright owner.

A CIP catalogue record is available from the
British Library.

ISBN 978 1 40534 707 5

Within each Top 10 list in this book, no
hierarchy of quality or popularity is implied.
All 10 are, in the editor's opinion, of roughly
equal merit.

Contents

Top 10 of Brussels, Bruges, Antwerp & Ghent

The information in this DK Eyewitness Top 10 Travel Guide is checked regularly
Every effort has been made to ensure that this book is as up-to-date as possible at the time
of going to press. Some details, however, such as telephone numbers, opening hours,
prices, gallery hanging arrangements and travel information are liable to change. The
publishers cannot accept responsibility for any consequences arising from the use of this
book, nor for any material on third party websites, and cannot guarantee that any website
address in this book will be a suitable source of travel information. We value the views and
suggestions of our readers very highly. Please write to: Publisher, DK Eyewitness Travel
Guides, Dorling Kindersley, 80 Strand, London WC2R 0RL, Great Britain.

Cover: Front – **DK Images:** Demitrio Carrasco clb; **Getty Images:** Taxi/David Noton main. Spine – **DK Images:**
Demetrio Carrasco b. Back – **DK Images:** Demetrio Carrasco cc, cr; Paul Kenward c.

Share your travel recommendations on traveldk.com

Left **Den Engel, a typical *bruine kroeg* (brown pub) in Antwerp** Right **Canal trip, Bruges**

Left **The Markt, Bruges** Right **The Brabo Fountain, Grote Markt, Antwerp**

TOP 10 OF BRUSSELS, BRUGES, ANTWERP & GHENT

ᵀᴼᴾ10 Highlights

The four great cities of northern Belgium share a rich cultural heritage dating back to medieval times, when this was one of the most vibrant trading regions in the world. Yet each is very different: Brussels is the new Capital of Europe, while Bruges is one of Europe's best preserved medieval cities. Ghent is a historic university city, while Antwerp still has the muscular stance of a great industrial centre. Each, in its own way, is richly rewarding – not only in cultural sights, but also in delightful and welcoming places to stay, eat and drink.

1 Grand Place, Brussels

For sheer architectural theatre, the historic centrepiece of Brussels is hard to beat – as it must have been three centuries ago *(see pp8–11)*.

2 Musées Royaux des Beaux-Arts, Brussels

Brueghel, Rubens, Van Dyke, Magritte – this splendid collection takes the visitor on a tour of some of the greatest names in art *(see pp12–15)*.

3 Musée des Instruments de Musique, Brussels

Newly rehoused in a magnificent Art Nouveau building, the "MIM" contains thousands of instruments – ancient, modern, ethnic and just plain wacky *(see pp16–17)*.

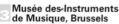

4 Musée Horta, Brussels

Victor Horta was the original Art Nouveau architect; his own house was the perfect expression of his art – down to the last doorknob. The building is now preserved as a shrine to Art Nouveau *(see pp18–19)*.

5 Centre Belge de la Bande Dessinée, Brussels

The "Comic Strip Centre" reveals all about this very Belgian art form: Tintin and beyond *(see pp20–21)*.

Preceding pages **Bruges: view from the Belfort on to the Rozenhoedkaai**

Central Brussels

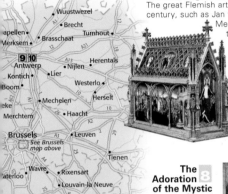

The Burg, Bruges

The old centre of Bruges is an architectural gem – a small, intimate square surrounded by historic buildings, each one offering something of fascination (see pp22–3).

Groeningemuseum and Memlingmuseum, Bruges

The great Flemish artists of the early 15th century, such as Jan van Eyck and Hans Memling, were among the first to perfect oil painting. These two unrivalled collections demonstrate conclusively their extraordinary skills, and show why they had such a profound influence on Italian art (see pp24–5).

The Adoration of the Mystic Lamb, Ghent

This large, multi-panel altarpiece created in 1426–32 by Jan van Eyck and his brother Hubrecht remains one of the great cultural treasures of Europe (see pp26–7).

Antwerp Cathedral

Antwerp's Cathedral of Our Lady is the city's main landmark, and the largest Gothic church in Belgium. Originating in the 14th century, its impressive interior is enhanced by two exceptional triptychs by Rubens: *The Raising of the Cross* and *The Descent from the Cross* (see pp28–9).

Rubenshuis, Antwerp

Rubens' mansion has been carefully restored to show how it might have been when he lived here (see pp30–31).

☝10 The Grand Place, Brussels

Brussels' Grand Place is the focal point of the city, a tirelessly uplifting masterpiece of unified architecture. Flanked by tightly packed rows of former guildhouses, bristling with symbolic sculpture and gilding, for many centuries this was the proud economic and administrative heart of the city. It was the setting for markets and fairs, pageants and jousts, for the proclamation of decrees, and public executions. Even without its old political and economic prestige and the bustle of through-traffic, it still throbs with animation.

Hôtel de Ville – detail of the façade

🍴 There are two famous bar-restaurants in the Grand Place – both pricey, but worth it for their utterly Bruxellois sense of style: Le Roy d'Espagne at No 1, and La Chaloupe d'Or at Nos 24–5.

ℹ Brussels' main tourist office is located in the Hôtel de Ville and is a useful place to pick up information.

• Map C3
• Hôtel de Ville: guided tours start 1:45–3.15pm Tue & Wed, 10–12.15pm Sun (1 Apr–31 Sep only). 02 279 4365. Tour: €2.50
• Maison du Roi (Musée de la Ville de Bruxelles): open 10am–5pm Tue–Sun. 02 279 4358. Admission: €2.50 •
Musée du Cacao et du Chocolat (off the Grand Place): open 10am–4:30pm Tue–Sun. 02 514 2048. Admission: €5 •
Maison des Brasseurs (Musée de la Brasserie): open 10am–5pm Mon–Fri, 12–5pm Sat & Sun. 02 511 4987. Adm: €4

Top 10 Sights
1. Hôtel de Ville
2. Maison du Roi
3. Le Renard
4. Le Cornet
5. The Tapis de Fleurs
6. Maison des Ducs de Brabant
7. Maison des Brasseurs
8. Le Cygne
9. Statue of Everard 't Serclaes
10. Maison des Boulangers

① Hôtel de Ville
The Town Hall was the first major building on the Grand Place. Largely reconstructed since its 15th-century beginnings, it still has its original spire, topped by a statue of St Michael killing the devil.

② Maison du Roi
This medieval-style "King's House" *(above)*, built in the 1870s, houses the Musée de la Ville de Bruxelles, a miscellany of city history, including costumes designed for the Manneken-Pis statue.

③ Le Renard
Like most of the buildings on the Grand Place, No 7 was a guildhouse – the prestigious headquarters of the Guild of Haber-dashers. Along with the majority of the guildhouses, it was rebuilt after 1695. A striking statue of a fox *(Le Renard)* illustrates the building's old name.

 For more on the Manneken-Pis See p10

4 Le Cornet
This gloriously elaborate building (No 6) was once the guildhouse of the boatmen. Its marine adornments include a top storey resembling the stern of a galleon.

The Grand Place

7 Maison des Brasseurs
Called L'Arbre d'Or (the Golden Tree), the brewers' guildhouse (No 10) was designed by Guillaume de Bruyn. It is still used by the Confédération des Brasseries de Belgique, and contains a small museum of brewing.

10 Maison des Boulangers
The bakers' guildhouse *(above)* is coated with symbols, including six figures representing the essential elements of breadmaking. The unusual octagonal lantern on the roof is topped by a striking gilded statue of Fame.

8 Le Cygne
"The Swan" (No 9) was rebuilt as a private residence in 1698, but in 1720 it was acquired by the Guild of Butchers. It later became a café, and Karl Marx held meetings of the German Workers' Party here.

5 The Tapis de Fleurs
Every other year for five days in mid-August, the Grand Place is taken over by a massive floral display known as the Carpet of Flowers *(above)*.

6 Maison des Ducs de Brabant
The south-eastern flank of this impressive Neo-Classical building was conceived (in 1698) as a single block of seven units by Guillaume de Bruyn.

9 Statue of Everard 't Serclaes
Everard 't Serclaes died on this site in 1388 resisting Flemish occupation. Passers-by stroke the limbs of his bronze statue *(below)* for luck.

Not quite the real thing
The guildhouses of the Grand Place are built largely in the Flemish Renaissance style of the late 16th and early 17th centuries. Little of it actually dates from this period, however. On 13–14 August 1695, under the orders of Louis XIV, French troops led by Marshal de Villeroy lined up their cannons, took aim at the spire of the Hôtel de Ville, and pulverized the city centre. In defiance, the citizens set about reconstructing the Grand Place, a task completed in just five years.

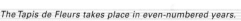

The Tapis de Fleurs takes place in even-numbered years.

Left **La Bourse** Centre **Église Saint-Nicholas** Right **Rue des Bouchers**

🔟 Around the Grand Place

Manneken-Pis
No one knows why this tiny bronze statue of a boy peeing a jet of water has become such a cherished symbol of Brussels, but it has. Since the early 18th century, costumes of all kinds have been made for him; he now has over 800. ◈ *corner of Rue de l'Étuve and Rue du Chêne • Map B3*

Galeries Royales de Saint-Hubert
Built in 1847, this was not the first shopping arcade in Europe, but it is certainly one of the most magnificent. ◈ *Map C2*

Rues des Bouchers
Many of the streets around the Grand Place reflect the trades that once operated there. The "Street of the Butchers" and its intersecting Petite Rue des Bouchers are famous for their lively restaurants and colourful displays of food. ◈ *Map C3*

Galeries Royales de Saint-Hubert

Église Saint-Nicholas
St Nicholas of Myra – a.k.a. Santa Claus – was the patron saint of merchants, and this church has served the traders of the Grand Place and surrounds since the 14th century. Its interior has retained an impressively medieval atmosphere, despite desecration by Protestant rebels in the 16th century, damage during the bombardment of 1695, and rebuilding in the 1950s. ◈ *Rue au Beurre 1 • Map C3 • 02 219 75 30 • Open 8am–6:30pm Mon–Fri, 9am–6pm Sat, 9am–7:30pm Sun • Free*

La Bourse
The Stock Exchange is an unmistakable feature of the Brussels landscape – built in 1873 like a Greek temple and lavishly decorated. It is now used by Euronext (European stock markets) and functions as an occasional exhibition space. Beneath it are the exposed archaeological remains of a convent founded in 1278, known as Bruxella 1278. ◈ *Map B3 • Bruxella 1278: 02 279 43 55. Guided tours first Wed of month (10:15am for tours in English)*

Musée du Costume et de la Dentelle
This small but surprisingly rewarding museum dedicated to historic costume and lace has a limited but choice selection of exhibits. ◈ *Rue de la Violette 12 • Map C3 • 02 213 44 50 • Open 10am–12:30pm & 1:30–5pm Mon–Fri; 2–5pm Sat–Sun • Admission charge*

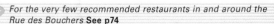

For the very few recommended restaurants in and around the Rue des Bouchers **See p74**

Biscuiterie Dandoy

Brussels' best makers of biscuits (cookies) have been perfecting their craft since 1829. Behind a ravishing shop window lie goodies such as *speculoos*, *sablés* and waffles. ◈ *Rue au Beurre 31 • Map C3*

Église Notre-Dame de Bon Secours

The most striking feature of this delightful little church, built in 1664–94, is its soaring hexagonal choir, rising to a domed ceiling. The façade bears the coat of arms of the enlightened 18th-century governor of the Austrian Netherlands, Charles of Lorraine. ◈ *Rue du Marché au Charbon 91 • Map B3 • 02 514 31 13 • Open daily Jun–Nov: 9:30am–6pm, Dec–May: 10am–5pm • Free*

Wedding dress, Musée du Costume

Place Saint-Géry

The square that marks the site of Brussels' first settlement is today dominated by Les Halles de Saint-Géry, an attractive iron and red-brick structure built in 1881 as a meat market. Now a craft market, exhibition space and café, it is the central focus of an area known increasingly for its nightlife. ◈ *Map B3*

Statue of Charles Buls

In Place Agora you will find one of Brussels' most delightful statues: a portrait of the splendidly bearded and moustachioed artist, scholar and reformer Charles Buls (1837–1914) and his dog. Buls, who served as Burgomaster from 1891 to 1899, is credited with restoring the Grand Place. ◈ *Map C3*

The Île Saint-Géry and the River Senne

Brussels began as a group of little islands on a marshy river. Legend has it that in the 6th century AD, St Géry, Bishop of Cambrai, founded a church on one of these islands, and a settlement grew around it. The name Bruocsella (later Brussels), meaning "house in the swamp", is first mentioned in 966, and a castle was built on the island by Charles, Duke of Lorraine, a decade later, effectively launching the city. There was a chapel on the island until 1798, when it was finally destroyed by occupying French revolutionary forces. The river, called the Senne, ran through the city until the 19th century, approximately along the line between the Gare du Midi and the Gare du Nord. Never large, it became overwhelmed by the growing population, and such a

The River Senne by Jean-Baptiste van Moer

health hazard that following another outbreak of cholera, it was covered over in 1867–71. This process created the Boulevard Anspach and the Boulevard Adolphe Max, among others, while the river formed part of the city's new sewer and drainage system. It can still be glimpsed here and there in the city.

 For more about Brussels' sewer system **See p40 (Musée des Égouts)**

Musées Royaux des Beaux-Arts

Brussels' "Royal Museums of the Fine Arts" are a tour de force. Many of the greatest names in art history are represented here – remarkably, they are predominantly home-grown. The museums are divided into three closely integrated parts, the Musée d'Art Ancien (15th to 18th centuries), the Musée d'Art Moderne (19th to 20th centuries) and the Musée Magritte, between which you can move freely. The museums are currently undergoing a major renovation which means that some exhibits might have been moved.

Musées Royaux des Beaux-Arts, façade

🖵 The Museums have their own good cafeteria. Far more exciting, however, is, MIM on top of the nearby Musée des Instruments de Musique *(see pp16–17)*; and just a short walk away are the cafés of the Place du Grand Sablon, including the exquisite *chocolatier* Wittamer *(see p72)*.

⏰ The 15th-, 16th- and 19th-century sections of the Museums close from noon–1pm; the 17th-, 18th- and 20th-century from 1–2pm – so plan accordingly.

• Rue de la Régence 3
• Map C4
• 02 508 32 11
• www.fine-arts-museum.be
• Open 10am–5pm Tues–Sun
• Admission €5 (under 13s free). Free admission on 1st Wed of each month after 1pm

Top 10 Works

1. The Justice of Othon
2. Lamentation
3. The Fall of Icarus
4. The Martyrdom of St Livincus
5. The Death of Marat
6. Les Masques Singuliers
7. Du Silence
8. The Promenade
9. Woman in Blue before a Mirror
10. The Domain of Arnheim

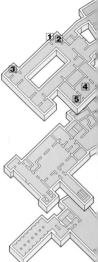

The Justice of Othon
This snapshot of brutal medieval life painted by Dirk Bouts (c.1420–75) in 1471–73, is a tale told in two panels – a kind of early comic strip. With brilliant clarity and detail, it depicts how Emperor Othon (Otto II) was fooled by his wife into beheading an innocent man for adultery.

Lamentation
Rogier van der Weyden was known for the disturbing emotional charge of his work, as in this painting of c.1420–50 of the crucified Christ in his mother's arms *(right)*.

The Fall of Icarus
This work of 1567 *(above)* by Pieter Brueghel the Elder wryly upstages the drama with prettified normality.

The Martyrdom of St Livincus
At his best, Rubens created works of staggering dynamism, compelling the eye to move through the painting, and inspiring a sense of exhilaration and awe. The savagery of this depiction of cruel martyrdom also conveys the power of redemption.

For more about the most famous Belgian artists See pp36–37

The Death of Marat 5
The French revolutionary Marat was murdered in his bath by a female assassin. This portrait *(right)* by Jacques-Louis David is strikingly realistic.

Woman in Blue before a Mirror 9
Rik Wouters' charm lies in the domestic intimacy of his interiors. The brush-strokes are energetic, the colours Fauvist – yet they have a rare delicacy and balance. This painting of 1914 shows his mastery of composition and colour.

Les Masques Singuliers 6
This powerful painting of 1892 *(right)* encapsulates the expressive, bizarre visual world and free-roaming imagination of the Belgian Symbolist artist James Ensor.

The Domain of Arnheim 10
René Magritte poses visual conundrums. In this painting of 1962 *(below)*, ambiguous feelings of threat and protection are suggested simultaneously.

Key
- Blue route
- Brown route
- Musée Magritte
- Green route

Du Silence 7
This beautifully executed, strangely alluring work of 1890 *(left)* is by Fernand Khnopff who was an influential Symbolist artist. He was concerned with delving into the uncharted world of the imagination.

The Promenade 8
This marvellous Pointillist scene of 1901 by Théo van Rysselberghe shows four girls walking along a windy beach.

Gallery Guide
The museums' collections are arranged by centuries, each with its own colour code. The Blue route covers the 15th and 16th, while the Brown features the 17th and 18th. The Musée Magritte houses the largest collection of the artist's work, including paintings, photographs, letters and drawings, while the descending levels of the Green route (levels -3 to -8) progress through 19th- and 20th-century art to the present day.

For more on the Belgian Symbolists **See p15**

Left **Main entrance hall** Centre *La Belle Captive*, Magritte Right **View of main galleries**

🔟 Beaux-Arts: Features and Collection

1 The Buildings
Set on the crest of the Coudenberg, the old royal enclave of Brussels, the museum's main buildings were designed by one of the leading architects of the day, Alphonse Balat (1818–95). He is also famous for designing the magnificent royal greenhouses at Laeken *(see p80)*, and for having taught Victor Horta *(see pp18–19)*.

2 Blue Route
The earliest rooms contain enough 15th- and 16th-century work for an entire visit. The creations of the early Flemish oil painters (the so-called "Primitives") shows the influence of the medieval manuscript illuminators; later works reveal the increasing influence of the Italian Renaissance.

3 The Brueghel Collection
The Blue route also includes the world's second largest collection of work by Pieter Brueghel the Elder, which hang alongside paintings by his son Pieter Brueghel the Younger, many of which were copied from his father's work.

4 Brown Route
Flemish painting had its second golden age in the 17th century, with such figure as Rubens, Jordaens and Van Dyck. This section shows why Antwerp was a key centre of European art in this period.

5 The Rubens Collection
Part of the Brown route, the Rubens collection shows why this painter was so fêted. To those who think of Rubens only in terms of scenes filled with plump, pink, naked ladies, this collection comes as a revelation, displaying vigour, spontaneity and artistic risk-taking.

6 Modern Belgian Art
The Green route ends with works by such iconoclastic modern artists as Marcel Broodthaers (1924–76), whose conceptual pieces reveal a very Belgian obsession with mussel shells, and Panamarenko (b.1940) whose work is represented by a typically bizarre flying machine.

7 Magritte Museum
The work of René Magritte is so often seen in reproduction that it may come as a surprise to see it up close. The impressive Magritte Museum, which is located in a separate section of the Musées Royaux des Beaux-Arts, houses the world's largest collection of the artist's work.

8 19th-Century Collection
This collection highlights the vigour and brilliance of Belgian art from the 1870s on, featuring work by artists such as Hippolyte Boulenger, Alfred Stevens, Charles Hermans, Henri Evenepoel and Émile Claus. The real stars here are the Symbolists and James Ensor.

Musées Royaux des Beaux-Arts is undergoing major renovations so some exhibits may change.

Green Route
The 20th-century and modern section includes international stars such as Picasso, Chagall and Dali. Belgium is also well represented, with work by Delvaux, Spilliaert, Wouters and several others.

Marché d'oranges à Blidah by Henri Evenepoel

Sint-Martens-Latem School
The work of Georges Minne, Gustave van de Woestyne, Albert Servaes, Valerius de Saedeleer,

Gustave de Smet and Constant Permeke covers a broad stylistic spectrum; the Green route offers a first-rate opportunity to see it.

The Belgian Symbolists

One of the great treasures of the Musées Royaux des Beaux-Arts is its collection of work by the Belgian Symbolists (mostly found on the Green route). Symbolism became the dominant sentiment of the last two decades of the 19th century. Initially a literary movement, its mood can be most readily detected in painting. Essentially, it was a reaction to Realism: rather than painting images of the world as it really appears, the Symbolists attempted to explore the world of the mind and imagination. Stylistically, Symbolism had a huge range: Jean Delville is famous for his highly charged mythic scenes; Fernand Khnopff uses cool draughtsmanship to evoke strange, unspoken tensions; many of Léon Spilliaert's works, composed in black and white, employ a highly original sense of design to evoke a powerful melancholic mood; Léon Frédéric moves seamlessly between powerful social realism and poetic Symbolism.

Baigneuse by Léon Spilliaert

Top 10 Forces in Belgian Symbolism

1 Fernand Khnopff (1858–1921)
2 Léon Frédéric (1856–1940)
3 Jean Delville (1867–1953)
4 Léon Spilliaert (1881–1946)
5 Théo Van Rysselberghe (1862–1926)
6 Félicien Rops (1833–98)
7 James Ensor (1860–1949)
8 George Minne (1866–1944)
9 Le Cercle des Vingt (1884–93)
10 La Libre Esthétique (1894–1914)

Musée des Instruments de Musique

The Musée des Instruments de Musique, often referred to as "Le MIM", has a supreme collection of musical instruments from ancient to modern. The exhibits – selected from a collection totalling more than 6,000 pieces – have recently been beautifully rearranged, and headphones permit visitors to hear what the instruments actually sound like. Added to this, the museum is housed in an exhilarating location: the classic Art Nouveau department store called "Old England". When you need refreshment, you can go up to the Café MIM on the top floor, which has one of the best views over Brussels.

The "Old England" building housing "Le MIM"

🍴 MIM, on the top floor of the museum, serves refreshments of all kinds, plus reasonably-priced light lunch dishes such as *focaccia*, sandwiches, pasta and a selection of salads. If this is too busy, you can always head off for the cafés of the Place du Grand Sablon, just a short walk away.

⏱ You should expect to spend at least two hours in this museum; to do it full justice, give it three to four hours. Note that although the Museum officially closes at 5pm, staff like to empty the exhibition rooms by 4:45pm.

• Rue Montagne de la Cour 2
• Map D4
• 02 545 01 30
• www.mim.fgov.be
• Open 9:30am–5pm Tue–Thu, 10am–5pm Sat–Sun • Admission: €5

Top 10 Features

1. The "Old England" Building
2. The Infrared Headphones
3. 20th-century Instruments
4. Mechanical Instruments
5. Non-European Instruments
6. Stringed Instruments
7. The Historical Survey
8. MIM Café-restaurant
9. European Folk Instruments
10. Keyboard Instruments

1 The "Old England" Building

Completed in 1899, this is a classic example of the innovative iron-and-glass structures produced by Art Nouveau architects. When visiting the MIM, make sure to look at the interior of the museum itself.

2 The Infrared Headphones

Infrared headphones are issued to all ticket holders; as you approach selected exhibits, recordings of those instruments are automatically triggered – which is both pleasurable and informative.

3 20th-century Instruments

Technology has had a major impact on music in recent decades, from electric amplification to synthesizers and, latterly, computer-generated music. This small collection offers a fascinating snapshot. If you don't know what an *ondes martenot* is, here's your chance to find out.

4 Mechanical Instruments

The ingenuity of instrument-makers is evident in this collection, which includes some outrageously elaborate musical boxes and a *carillon* – a set of bells used to play tunes.

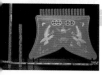

5 Non-European Instruments

The MIM runs a strong line in ethnomusicology. This impressive collection includes panpipes, sitars, African harps and drums, gamelan orchestras, and giant Tibetan horns.

8 MIM Café-restaurant

Even if you don't need refuelling, take the lift up to the 10th floor to admire the view. From here you can see the statue of St Michael glistening on the top of the spire of the Hôtel de Ville in the Grand Place, and far across town to the Basilique Nationale and the Atomium.

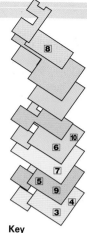

6 Stringed Instruments

Sharing the 2nd floor is the stringed instrument section, including violins of all shapes and sizes, psalteries, dulcimers, harps, lutes and guitars. There is also a reconstruction of a violin-maker's workshop.

7 The Historical Survey

This section charts the evolution of western "art" instruments from antiquity through the Renaissance to the 19th century. The headphone guide shows the evolving complexity of musical sound.

9 European Folk Instruments

This fascinating collection includes pipes, rattles, accordions, hurdy-gurdies and some splendid oddities – chief among them a collection of Belgian glass trumpets.

10 Keyboard Instruments

Star exhibits include harpsichords by the Ruckers family *(below)*, who worked in Antwerp from the 16th century.

Key

	Basement (-1)
	First floor
	Second floor
	Fourth floor
	Fifth floor
	Seventh floor
	Eighth floor
	Tenth floor

Museum Guide

The museum is set out on five of the building's ten floors. Floor –1 is devoted to mechanical and 20th-century instruments. The first floor covers folk instruments. The historical survey of western musical instruments begins on the 2nd floor and continues on the 4th floor, where the keyboard and stringed instruments are concentrated. There is a library (access by appointment) on the 5th floor and a concert hall on the 8th; the café-restaurant is on the top floor. The floors are connected by stairs and a lift.

For more on Art Nouveau architecture in Brussels
See pp44–5

TOP 10 Musée Horta, Brussels

In the late 19th century, Brussels was a centre for avant-garde design, and a rapidly growing city. To feed the market for stylish mansions, architects scavenged history for ideas; the result was the so-called "eclectic style". In 1893, the gifted architect Victor Horta created a totally new style – later labelled "Art Nouveau" – full of sensuous curves and artistic surprises, elaborated with wrought iron, stained glass, mosaics, murals and finely crafted woodwork. Horta brought this style to full maturity when he built his own house – now the Musée Horta.

The Salon, Musée Horta

There are several interesting bars and cafés nearby, around Place du Châtelain. For a spot of good-value lunch before the museum's 2pm opening hour, try the charming La Canne en Ville *(see p81)*; for somewhere with real design flair, head for the extraordinary Quincaillerie, which dates from 1903 *(see p81)*.

The Musée Horta is at the heart of a cluster of Art Nouveau buildings. Key streets include Rue Defacqz, Rue Faider and Rue Paul-Émile Janson. Hôtel Hannon is also close by *(see pp44–5)*.

- Rue Américaine 23–25, Brussels 1060 (Saint-Gilles)
- Map G2
- 02 543 04 90
- www.hortamuseum.be
- Open 2–5:30pm Tue–Sun. Closed Mon, public hols
- Admission: €7

Top 10 Features

1. The Building
2. The Staircase
3. Structural Ironwork
4. Fixtures and Fittings
5. Furniture
6. Leaded Glass
7. Mosaics
8. Woodwork
9. Philippe Wolfers Collection
10. Scale Model of the Volkshuis

1 The Building

When designing houses for clients, Horta liked to study how they lived, and tailor the house accordingly. His own house is designed in two distinct parts: on the left (from the outside), his residence; on the right, his offices and studio.

2 The Staircase

The interior design hangs on a central stairwell, lit from the top by a large, curving skylight. The ironwork bannisters have been given a typically exuberant flourish *(above)*.

3 Structural Ironwork

In what was considered a bold gesture at the time, Horta used iron structures to support his houses. He even made a virtue of it, by leaving some of the iron exposed and drawing attention to it with wrought-iron embellishments *(below)*.

For more of Horta's Art Nouveau buildings **See pp44–5**

4 Fixtures and Fittings

Horta was an *ensemblier*: he liked to design an entire building in all its detail, down to the last light fixture, door handle and coat hook. This attention to detail conveys the impression of complete architectural mastery: nothing is left to chance.

7 Mosaics

The sinuous lines of Art Nouveau design in the mosaic tiling of the dining room floor *(above)* help to soften the effect of the white-enamelled industrial brick lining the walls.

9 Philippe Wolfers Collection

Horta worked with a leading jeweller and silversmith of the day, Philippe Wolfers (1858–1929). Using typically sensuous, lavish designs, Wolfers combined gems, ivory and precious metals to create not only jewellery, but also houseware items such as lamps and ornaments. A selection of his work is on display in Horta's office *(below)*.

10 Scale Model of the Volkshuis

Although few have survived, Horta was well-known for his designs for commercial and public buildings. The Volkshuis (La Maison du Peuple), was an innovative cast-iron structure built for the Société Coopérative in 1895. A scale model of it can be seen in the cellar.

5 Furniture

In addition to door handles and coat hooks, Horta also liked to design the furniture to go in his houses. Although it bears a definite Art Nouveau stamp, Horta's furniture tends to be simple, restrained and practical.

8 Woodwork

There is a note of austerity as well as luxury in Art Nouveau design. The richly carved wood in the dining room is left natural, allowing the quality of the wood to speak for itself *(below)*.

Victor Horta

The son of a Ghent shoemaker, Victor Horta (1861–1947) studied architecture from the age of 13. After designing the Hôtel Tassel *(see page 44)* in 1893, his reputation soared. Thereafter he designed houses, department stores and public buildings. With World War I, Art Nouveau fell from favour, and Horta turned to a harder style, seen in his Palais des Beaux-Arts in Brussels. He was awarded the title of Baron in 1932.

6 Leaded Glass

The nature of leaded glass – glass shapes held together by lead strips – stimulated the artistic flair of Art Nouveau architects. It appears at various points in the house – notably the door panels and stairwell skylight.

TOP 10 Centre Belge de la Bande Dessinée

We've all heard of Tintin – perhaps the most famous Belgian in the world. But this comic-strip hero is just one of hundreds produced in Belgium over the last century. The comic strip – bande dessinée in French – is called the "ninth art". The library at Brussels' Centre Belge de la Bande Dessinée contains 40,000 volumes – it's taken that seriously. Set out in a renovated fabric warehouse, the CBBD (pronounced cébébédé) presents the history of the form, shows how strips are made, and explores some of the key characters and their creators.

Brasserie Horta

🄰 The CBBD's own **Brasserie Horta** is a convenient place for refreshments, and serves a good range of lunch dishes. If that doesn't appeal, you are only a short walk from the Grand Place and its multitude of cafés and restaurants. Nearer at hand is the famous bar **A la Mort Subite** *(see p72)*, a traditional place to sample *gueuze* beer.

🄲 Note that the CBBD is *not* guaranteed to entertain small children, especially if they do not speak French or Dutch. It is, rather, a museum showing the evolution of the craft. There are free guides in English.

- Rue des Sables 20
- Map D2
- 02 219 19 80
- www.cbbd.be
- Open 10am–6pm Tue–Sun
- Admission: €7.50

Top 10 Features

1. The Building
2. How Comic Strips Are Made
3. Espace Saint-Roch
4. Comic Book Themes
5. Library
6. Le Musée de l'Imaginaire
7. Le Musée de la Bande Dessinée Moderne
8. Slumberland Bookshop
9. Audio-visual Room
10. Tintin

1 The Building

The CBBD occupies what was formerly the Magasins Wauquez, an innovative Art Nouveau structure of cast iron supporting large expanses of glass, designed by Victor Horta in 1903–6 *(main image) (see p45)*.

2 How Comic Strips Are Made

This small exhibit deals with the practicalities of the art: how the imagination of the story-writer and artist-designer *(le scénariste)* is converted into a visual form and prepared for printing.

3 Espace Saint-Roch

A large, darkened exhibition space is filled with display cases where 200 of the 6,000 or so original pieces of artwork in the museum's collection are displayed in rotation. Many were rescued from the publishers' wastepaper baskets – formerly their usual fate after publication.

4 Comic Book Themes

The second floor of the museum is where a variety of temporary exhibitions are hosted. These are organized throughout the year and are always related to a special comic book theme or artist.

8 Slumberland Bookshop

Named after the Little Nemo adventure, the shop stocks everything on the comic strip theme.

5 Library

The library *(above)* has a public reading room, which is open to anyone with a museum ticket.

9 Audio-visual Room

This small room is used primarily to show films related to the temporary exhibitions.

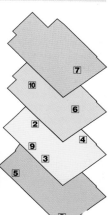

Museum floorplan

Key

■	Ground floor
■	First floor
■	Second floor
■	Third floor

6 Le Musée de l'Imaginaire

The "Museum of the Imagination" traces the origins of the comic strip, and looks at many of the classic characters.

7 Le Musée de la Bande Dessinée Moderne

This exhibit *(below)* looks at recent comic-strip trends, including humorous, political and erotic work.

10 Tintin

Of course, the main hero of the CBBD is the famous boy-reporter Tintin *(above)*, creation of Hergé. Translated into some 40 languages, over 140 million copies of the books have been sold worldwide. The museum acknowledges his status with 3-D models of key characters, and the rocket that went to the moon.

Tintin

The story of Tintin goes back to 1929, when he first appeared in a children's newspaper supplement *Le Petit Vingtième*. His Brussels-born inventor Hergé (Georges Rémi, *see p48*) developed the character as he took him through a series of adventures related to real events, such as the rise of fascism (*King Ottakar's Sceptre*). The enduring charm of Tintin is his naive determination, as well as the multitude of archetypal characters that surround him, such as Captain Haddock, Professor Calculus and, of course, Tintin's faithful dog Snowy.

For more about Hergé See p48

⟲10 The Burg, Bruges

Bruges began life in about AD 862 as a castle on an island in a swamp formed by the River Reie. The castle has disappeared, but the charming square that replaced it, the Burg, has remained the historic heart of the city over the centuries. The most impressive building is the Stadhuis, a classic late-medieval town hall built when Bruges was a hub of international trade. Just about every century is represented by the buildings on the Burg, and visiting them discloses many of the fascinating secrets that lie behind this extraordinary city.

Breidelstraat

🍴 Tom Pouce, right on the Burg, is good for coffee, drinks and waffles.

🔆 All the sights in the Burg are high in quality but small in content. You can see everything in an hour or two.

- Map L4
- Heilig Bloedbasiliek/ St Basil's Chapel. Burg 13 Open Apr–Sep: 9:30–noon & 2–6pm daily; Oct–Mar: 10–noon & 2–6pm Thu–Tue, 2–4pm Wed. Admission to Schatkamer (museum): €1.50
- Stadhuis ("Gothic Hall"). Burg 12 Open 9:30am–5pm daily. Admission: €2.50 (inc. audioguide and entrance to Renaissancezaal; children under 13 free)
- Renaissancezaal van het Brugse Vrije. Burg 11a Open 9:30am–12:30pm & 1:30–5pm Tue–Sun. Admission: included in admission price for Stadhuis

Top 10 Sights

1. Breidelstraat
2. Heilig Bloedbasiliek
3. St Basil's Chapel
4. Stadhuis
5. Oude Griffie
6. Renaissancezaal van het Brugse Vrije
7. Landhuis van het Brugse Vrije
8. The North Side
9. Proostdij
10. Blinde Ezelstraat

Breidelstraat
The quaint little street *(above left)* that connects Bruges' main market place, the Markt, to the Burg is lined with shops selling souvenirs as well as one of the city's most famous products, lace.

Heilig Bloedbasiliek
On the west side of the Burg lies the Basilica of the Holy Blood *(above)*, a chapel lavishly restored in Neo-Gothic style in the late 19th century. Its tiny museum holds its most famous relic, a phial of blood said to be Christ's.

St Basil's Chapel
Beneath the Heilig Bloedbasiliek is another chapel of an utterly contrasting mood *(below)*. Constructed of hefty grey stone in the 12th century, it is a superb and atmospheric example of muscular Romanesque style, and a reminder of the Burg's origins as a castle.

For more on Bruges' famous festival, the Heilig Bloedprocessie See p50

Stadhuis

One of medieval Europe's great secular buildings *(main image)*, the Stadhuis (town hall) is a magnificent expression of Bruges' self-confidence in medieval times, built in 1376–1420 in aptly named Flamboyant Gothic style. It was much restored in the late 19th century.

Landhuis van het Brugse Vrije

This sober 18th-century mansion was the headquarters of the "Liberty of Bruges", which was an administrative jurisdiction covering a large region around the city, while Bruges governed itself separately.

Plan of the Burg

Blinde Ezelstraat

A picturesque street leads off from the south of the Burg, beneath the arch that links the Oude Griffie to the Stadhuis. The name "Blind Donkey St" may relate to a nearby inn famed for its cheap beer.

Oude Griffie

The Renaissance touched Bruges' architecture only lightly; this "Old Recorders' House", built in 1534–7 *(below)*, is the exception.

The North Side

This ultra-modern Pavilion *(above)* by Toyo Ito was built in 2002 on the site of the "missing" cathedral *(see panel)*, to mark Bruges' year as a Cultural Capital of Europe.

Renaissancezaal van het Brugse Vrije

In the corner of the Burg is the Renaissance Room, whose star exhibit is the Charles V Chimneypiece, a virtuoso piece of 16th-century wood carving.

Proostdij

The Provost's House lining the north side of the Burg is in Flemish Baroque style (1622), with a roofline balustrade topped by the figure of Justice.

The Missing Cathedral

Images of the centre of Bruges before 1799 show the north side of the Burg occupied by the impressive hulk of the Sint-Donaaskerk. The first church on this site dated back to Bruges' origins, and Jan van Eyck was buried here. Gradually enlarged over the centuries, in 1559 it became the city's cathedral. But during the occupation by French revolutionary forces, it was demolished. Excavated parts of its foundations can still be seen in the Crowne Plaza hotel.

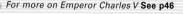

TOP 10 Two Museums of Bruges

These two museums contain some of the world's finest examples of late medieval art, presenting a treasured selection of work by artists such as Jan van Eyck (c.1390–1441) and Hans Memling (1435–94). The two museums are on separate sites, a short distance apart. The Groeningemuseum is a small and charming gallery with a radical edge. The Memlingmuseum is part of the old restored Sint-Janshospitaal – the medieval hospital that commissioned Memling's paintings for the very chapel in which they can still be seen.

Façade of the Groeningemuseum

- The Groeninge-museum is only a short walk from the centre of town, where there is a wide choice of cafés and restaurants *(see p91).*

- If you intend to see several of the Bruges museums, it's worth asking at the tourist office in the Burg if a Combination Ticket is available. Normally this allows the holder to visit five city museums – including these two – for about €15.

• Groeningemuseum: Dijver 12. Map L4. 050 44 87 11 Open 9:30am–5pm Tue–Sun. Admission: €8 (children under 13 free)

• Memlingmuseum: Mariastraat 38. Map K5 Open 9:30am–5pm Tue–Sun. Admission: €8 (children under 13 free)

Top 10 Paintings

1. The Last Judgment
2. The Judgment of Cambyses
3. The St Ursula Shrine
4. The Legend of St Ursula
5. The Moreel Triptych
6. Secret-Reflet
7. The Virgin and Child with Canon van der Paele
8. Portrait of a Bruges Family
9. The Triptych with Sts John the Baptist and John the Evangelist
10. The Adoration of the Magi

1 The Last Judgment
Hieronymus Bosch (c.1450–1516) is famous for his nightmarish paintings of spiritual anguish, torture and hell. This example *(above)* is a perplexing insight into the religious psyche of the times.

2 The Judgment of Cambyses
In 1488, Bruges ill-advisedly imprisoned Maximilian, governor of the Low Countries. This large diptych by Gerard David depicting the gruesome flaying of a corrupt judge *(right)* was commissioned for the town hall as a sort of public apology.

3 The St Ursula Shrine
Completed by Hans Memling in 1479, this metre-long reliquary *(above)* depicts the Legend of St Ursula in 14 exquisitely detailed panels.

The Legend of St Ursula

This series of panels by the "Master of the Saint Ursula Legend" tells the popular medieval tale of St Ursula and her company of 11,000 virgins, cruelly martyred in pagan Germany.

Secret-Reflet

This classic Symbolist work *(right)* of 1902 by Fernand Khnopff (1858–1921) includes an image of the Sint-Janshospitaal. The title refers to the play on the word "reflection" in the two images.

The Adoration of the Magi

This smaller work, also displayed in the chapel of the Memlingmuseum, is another painted by Memling in 1479. It is known as the Jan Floreins Triptych after the patron, seen kneeling on the left of the central panel.

The Virgin and Child with Canon van der Paele

The supreme masterpiece of the collection *(above)* was painted in 1436 by Jan van Eyck. The detail is astonishing.

Portrait of a Bruges Family

In the 17th century, Antwerp became the new centre of trade and culture; but Bruges still retained a certain level of prosperity and dignity, as witnessed in this family portrait by Jacob van Oost the Elder *(right)*.

The Golden Age of Bruges

Under the dukes of Burgundy Bruges prospered, and in 1429 it became the capital of the Burgundian empire. Its elite became wealthy, educated patrons of the arts. The dukes of Burgundy married into European royalty: Philip the Good married Isabella of Portugal; Charles the Bold, Margaret of York. Their marriages were celebrated with vast feasts – the stuff of European legends. This is the world glimpsed in the paintings of the Flemish masters.

The Moreel Triptych

Willem Moreel, the Burgomaster of Bruges, commissioned this work *(above)* from Hans Memling in 1484. Moreel is depicted in the left-hand panel, his wife in the right.

The Triptych with Sts John the Baptist and John the Evangelist

Painted by Memling in 1479, this work celebrates the two St Johns, patron saints of the Sint-Janshospitaal.

For Jacob van Oost's Portrait of a Bruges Family **See p84**

🔟 The Adoration of the Mystic Lamb

St Bavo's cathedral in Ghent is home to one of the greatest cultural treasures of northern Europe. This huge, exquisitely painted polyptych is the masterpiece of the brothers Hubrecht and Jan van Eyck. Its survival is something of a miracle. It was rescued from Protestant vandals in 1566, and from fire in 1822. Parts were carried off by French soldiers in 1794, sold in 1816, then stolen in 1934. The original has been reconstructed in its entirety, apart from the lower left panel (a modern copy). It is kept in the Vijd Chapel, named after its original patron.

Sint-Baafskathedraal
(Cathedral of St Bavo)

🅒 There are several friendly cafés immediately outside the cathedral. More spectacular, though, is the De Foyer café-restaurant on the first floor of the Schouwburg (theatre), with a terrace overlooking the square *(see p99)*.

🅒 Get there well before closing time: the Vijd Chapel shuts promptly. Last tickets are issued 15 minutes before closing; last audio-guides (which last 50 minutes), 30 minutes before closing.

• Sint-Baafskathedraal, Sint-Baafsplein
• Map Q2
• 09 269 20 45
• Open Apr–Oct: 9:30am–5pm Mon–Sat, 1–5pm Sun; Nov–Mar: 10:30am–4pm Mon–Sat, 1–4pm Sun
• Admission: €3, (6–12 yrs €1.50)

Top 10 Features

1. The Polyptych
2. The Mystic Lamb of God
3. God the Almighty
4. Flowers
5. Mary
6. The Angel-musicians
7. Eve
8. The Idealized City
9. The Inscription
10. The External Panels

1 The Polyptych
The painting consists of 12 panels, four in the centre and four on each of the folding wings. The lower tier depicts the spirituality of the world, and God's chosen people; the upper tier shows the heavenly realm with Adam and Eve on either end.

2 The Mystic Lamb of God
The focus of this panel *(above)* is the Lamb of God, spurting blood on an altar. Four sets of figures approach: virgin martyrs; figures from the New Testament and the Church; patriarchs and prophets of the Old Testament; and confessors of the Faith.

3 God the Almighty
The central figure of the upper tier is God, depicted in a brilliant red robe and a bejewelled mitre, carrying a sceptre and with a crown at his feet. The benign calm and poise of the face radiate throughout the polyptych.

The audioguide to the polyptych (available in several languages) is included in the ticket price. It is long, but extremely informative

4 Flowers
The numerous flowers make a philosophical point: everything in nature is an expression of God's work. The painter's job was to record it faithfully.

5 Mary
The figure of Mary tells us much about the concept of feminine beauty in medieval times. Fine-featured, absorbed in her reading, she is decked with jewels.

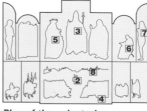

Plan of the polyptych

10 The External Panels
The wings of the painting can be closed. The external panels are tonally quite flat, intensifying the moment they are opened to reveal the sumptuous interior.

6 The Angel-musicians
A heavenly choir sings on one side of the upper tier *(right)*, while on the other, an orchestra of angels plays. The figures are tightly crowded, but the perspective is good.

7 Eve
Jan van Eyck's contemporaries were startled by the realism of his Adam and Eve. Even today, their nudity among the luxuriously clothed figures is striking. Beautifully lit from the right, they show the painter's profound understanding of the human form.

8 The Idealized City
To the rear of the central panel rise the towers and spires of the heavenly city, Jerusalem.

9 The Inscription
In the 19th century, a verse inscription by the two brothers, thought to be original, was uncovered on the frame.

Influence on European Art
Flemish painters, Jan van Eyck in particular, are sometimes credited with inventing oil painting. This is an exaggeration, but certainly they perfected the technique. Antonello da Messina, the Italian credited with pioneering oil painting in Italy, is believed to have learnt his skills from Flemish artists. As a result of these contacts, the advantages of oil painting over tempera or fresco became clear. Italian artists adopted oil painting, and Italian art accelerated toward the High Renaissance.

For more on St Bavo's cathedral **See p95**

🔟 Antwerp Cathedral

Antwerp Cathedral is the largest Gothic church in the Low Countries – also one of the most beautiful. Its dainty wedding-cake spire, rising up from a medieval market square, is still a major landmark in the city. The cathedral took 170 years to build, and even then was not complete. It was the church of the wealthy guilds, richly adorned with their shrines, reliquaries and altarpieces. Gutted by fire and vandals in the 16th and 18th centuries, the cathedral still has a number of major treasures, chief among them two magnificent triptychs by Rubens.

The West Door

🍴 There are plenty of cafés, bars and restaurants near the cathedral. One tavern, Het Vermoeide Model *(see p108)*, is actually built up against the cathedral walls. You can hear the organ from the terrace of the restaurant Rooden Hoed *(see p108)*. The bar Het Elfde Gebod (The Eleventh Commandment) is decorated with religious statuary *(see p109)*.

🎵 Listen out for the carillon bells – the set of 49 bells that play tunes on the hour. In the summer, regular carillon concerts are given, when the bells are played from a keyboard.

- Handschoenmarkt
- Map T2
- 03 213 99 51
- Open 10am–5pm Mon–Fri, 10am–3pm Sat, 1–4pm Sun and public hols
- Admission: €4, children under 12 free

Top 10 Features

1. The Spire
2. The Nave
3. The Raising of the Cross
4. The Pulpit
5. Original Murals
6. The Virgin Exalted through Art
7. The Burgundian Window
8. The Cupola
9. The Madonna of Antwerp
10. The Schyven Organ

The Spire

The cathedral's dainty and unusual spire was built over about 100 years from the mid 1400s onward. As it rises to its pinnacle at 123 m (404 feet) it shows increasingly daring Gothic style. The only other comparable spire is that of the Hôtel de Ville in Brussels, of a similar date.

The Nave

The interior is bright, light and uplifting, largely by virtue of its scale, the expanse of glass, and the simple, soaring space that rises to the rib vaults. Unusually, the columns of the aisle have no capitals, so bend seamlessly to form Gothic arches, creating a serene effect.

The Raising of the Cross

This triptych, and the equally impressive *Descent from the Cross* on the other side of the nave, secured Rubens' reputation in Antwerp. The central and right-hand panels display the dynamic energy that was Rubens' hallmark. The left-hand panel shows the grief of Christ's companions.

For more on Rubens See pp30–31

The Pulpit
Elaborately carved oak pulpits are a feature of many Belgian churches. The subject of this one, the propagation of the faith in the "four" continents, is tackled with extraordinary ambition – a riot of birds, trees, textile swags, angels, saints and symbolic figures.

Plan of the cathedral

The Virgin Exalted through Art
In the late 19th century, the cathedral was rescued from neglect by massive restoration. In some cases this was overzealous, but the effort to recreate a medieval effect in some of the chapels behind the choir is admirable. Albert de Vriendt's fine triptych shows the "Eyckian" revival at its best.

The Burgundian Window
A fair amount of the cathedral's original stained glass has survived. This is the oldest window, dating from 1503 (below). It depicts Philip the Handsome and Joanna of Castile, with their patron saints behind them.

Original Murals
The cathedral was once bright with murals, but over time they fell away or were overpainted. Restoration has revealed patches of the originals.

The Cupola
From outside, the dome looks like a tiered black onion. Inside (left), its logic is clear: the glass tiers let in light to illuminate the *Assumption of the Virgin* (1647), Cornelis Schut's impressive ceiling painting. The effect is of looking straight up into the heavens.

The Madonna of Antwerp
This exceptional little wooden statue has been a focus of devotion since the 16th century, and has a changing wardrobe of robes and crowns.

The Schyven Organ
This impressive instrument is housed in a magnificent 17th-century case created by three leading sculptors of the day.

Iconoclasts and French Revolutionaries
Antwerp Cathedral was once richly decorated; two episodes have rendered it rather more austere. The first, in the 1560s, was the onslaught of Protestant zealots, or "iconoclasts", who set about ridding churches of statues, paintings and relics. The second wave occurred in the 1790s, when the forces of the French Revolution went about demolishing churches, or putting them to secular use as stables, warehouses, barracks, law courts, and factories.

Rubenshuis, Antwerp

In 1610, Pieter Paul Rubens (1577–1640) – court painter, recently returned from Italy, and newly married – found himself in a position to buy a large house, where he lived and worked until his death. After centuries of neglect, the house was rescued by the City of Antwerp in 1937, and has since been refurbished and re-furnished to look as it might have done in Rubens' day. Quite apart from the sheer charm of the place, it provides a rare opportunity to see the physical context in which great works of art were made.

The gardens of the Rubenshuis

🅐 The Rubenshuis houses an elegant café-restaurant called Rubens Inn, serving snacks as well a substantial lunch menu. For a touch of modern style, the upbeat Grand Café Horta is just around the corner at Hopland 2 *(see p108).*

🅒 The museum gets very, very busy at peak times, all day, every day, especially in summer. For some chance of a quieter visit, arrive at opening time – although you may find scores of other people have had the same idea.

- Wapper 9–11
- Map U2
- 03 201 15 55
- http://museum. antwerpen.be/rubenshuis
- Open 10am–5pm Tue–Sun. Closed Mon and public hols.
- Admission: €6 (includes audioguide; ID needed as security). Free on last Wed of every month

Top 10 Features

1. The Building
2. The Baroque Portico
3. The Parlour Room
4. The Kitchen
5. The Art Gallery
6. The Dining Room
7. The Large Bedroom
8. The Semi-circular Museum
9. The Little Bedroom
10. Rubens' Studio

1 The Building
The house is in two parts set around an inner courtyard. As you enter, the older, Flemish-style half is to the left – a series of rooms providing the domestic quarters, where Rubens lived and entertained. To the right is the working part of the house, containing Rubens' studio and designed by the artist in grander Baroque style.

2 The Baroque Portico
The massive ornamental screen *(right)* was designed by Rubens in Italianate Baroque style to link the two parts of the house. It also provides a theatrical entrance to the formal garden beyond.

3 The Parlour Room
This room is notable for its wall hangings. Embossed Spanish leather was used as a kind of wallpaper in the houses of the well-to-do.

The Kitchen

This charming little kitchen, with its tiled walls and open fireplace, is typical of Flanders. Note the pothooks with ratchets, designed to adjust the height of cooking vessels over the fire. The robust traditions of Flemish cuisine were forged in such kitchens.

The Large Bedroom

Rubens died in this room, now refurbished as a living room. The beautiful curio cabinet seen here is decorated with mythological scenes based on Rubens' work.

Plan of the Rubenshuis

Key

- Ground floor
- First floor

The Semi-circular Museum

This elegant marble-lined room *(above)* inspired by the Pantheon in Rome was used by Rubens to exhibit his collection of sculpture. Among the pieces shown today is a bust of a Satyr attributed to Lucas Fayherbe.

Rubens' Studio

In this large and impressive room *(above)*, Rubens worked with a team of assistants and apprentices to maintain his huge productivity. Pictures shown here include the exhilarating but unfinished *Henry IV in the Battle of Ivry* (c.1628–30).

The Art Gallery

A painting exhibited here, *The Art Gallery of Cornelis van der Geest*, shows how Rubens' own gallery might have looked – every inch of wall space hung with pictures.

The Little Bedroom

The most eye-catching item in this room is the 17th-century box bed *(above)* in which people slept half sitting-up to promote good digestion.

The Dining Room

Eating and drinking played a central role in the social habits of Rubens' day *(right)*. A highlight here is a self-portrait of the artist *(main image)*, one of just four in existence.

Swagger and Verve

Rubens began training as an artist aged 13, but it was an eight-year stay in Italy that transformed him. His work chimed with the grandeur and swagger of Baroque architecture and the Counter-Reformation, also with the luxurious life style of the European aristocracy. Working with ceaseless energy, he produced over 2,000 major paintings in his lifetime.

The best collections of Rubens' work are in the fine arts museums of Brussels and Antwerp **See pp34–5**

Left **Sint-Janshospitaal (Memlingmuseum)** Right **Musée David et Alice van Buuren**

⑩ Art Galleries

1 Musées Royaux des Beaux-Arts, Brussels

Brussels' royal museum of fine art holds rich collections of Brueghel, Rubens, Jordaens and Wouters *(below)*, as well as some 200 works by Magritte in the Magritte Museum *(see pp12–15)*.

Woman in Blue Dress by Rik Wouters

2 Musée Communal d'Ixelles, Brussels

This small but rewarding collection of art boasts names like Rembrandt, Toulouse-Lautrec and Picasso, as well as leading Belgian artists such as Léon Spilliaert *(right)*. The museum is located in the borough of Ixelles, just south of the city centre *(see p78)*.

3 Musée Constantin Meunier, Brussels

The suburban home of the late-19th-century sculptor Constantin Meunier has been turned into a gallery devoted to his work; it leaves the visitor in no doubt of his gifts and the pungency of his social criticism *(see p79)*.

4 Musée David et Alice van Buuren, Brussels

A private collection of art is presented in its original setting: a charming Art Deco home with a beautiful garden *(see p77)*.

5 Groeningemuseum, Bruges

Bruges' main gallery is celebrated above all for its superb collection of paintings by Flemish Masters of the late medieval "Golden Age". A small, easily digestible museum *(see pp24–5)*.

6 Memlingmuseum, Bruges

A superb collection of paintings by Hans Memling was originally commissioned for the chapel of the medieval hospital, the Sint-Janshospitaal, to bring solace to the sick. Now the conjoining wards and chapel have been restored, giving these works a fascinating context *(see pp24–5)*.

Les Troncs Gris by Léon Spilliaert

7 Museum voor Schone Kunsten, Ghent

Ghent's recently renovated museum of fine arts is a bit of a mixed bag, but has a handful of outstanding pieces; just a stone's throw from SMAK, it forms part of a rewarding double act *(see p97)*.

8 Stedelijk Museum voor Actuele Kunst (SMAK), Ghent

This acclaimed gallery of contemporary art not only mounts cutting-edge temporary exhibitions, but also has a remarkable permanent collection. Guaranteed to provoke a reaction from aficionados and the unconverted alike *(see p97)*.

Stedelijk Museum voor Actuele Kunst

9 Koninklijk Museum voor Schone Kunsten, Antwerp

Antwerp's excellent fine arts museum has examples of the best of Belgian art, from Jan van Eyck to Pierre Alechinsky, placing it in the top rank of European collections *(see pp103)*.

10 Museum voor Hedendaagse Kunst (MUHKA), Antwerp

The location of this museum of contemporary art, in the up-and-coming former dockland area in the south of the city, sets the tone for what lies inside. A ground-breaking gallery with a growing reputation *(see p106)*.

Top 10 Works Outside Galleries

1 The Adoration of the Mystic Lamb (1432)
Jan and Hubrecht van Eyck's masterpiece *(see pp26–7)*.

2 The Raising of the Cross (1609–10)
Wonderful triptych by Pieter Paul Rubens *(see p28)*.

3 The Descent from the Cross (1611–14)
Rubens' heartrending triptych contrasts Christ's death with the Nativity *(see p28)*.

4 Madonna and Child (1504–5)
Michelangelo sculpture of mesmeric dignity *(see p86)*.

5 Baroque Pulpit (1699)
Hendrik Verbruggen's elaborately carved pulpit in Brussels' cathedral *(see p68)*.

6 The History of Bruges (1895)
In the Stadhuis of Bruges *(see pp22–3)*, 12 superb Neo-Medievalist murals by Albert and Julien De Vriendt.

7 The Thinker (c.1905)
A copy of Rodin's statue on a tomb in Laeken Cemetery, Brussels. ◈ *Parvis Notre-Dame, 1020 BRU (Laeken)* • *Map F1* • *Open 8:30am–4:30pm daily*

8 Fulfilment and The Dancer (1908–11)
Gustav Klimt's mosaic masterpieces in the dining room of the Palais Stoclet are rarely on public view *(see p80)*.

9 Fountain of Kneeling Youths (1898)
Georges Minne's best-known work. ◈ *Emile Braunplein (in front of the Belfort, Ghent)*

10 Nos Vieux Trams Bruxellois (1978)
Paul Delvaux's contribution to putting art in the metro. ◈ *Bourse Station, Brussels*

For more on the Belgian Symbolists See p15

Left *The Assumption* by Rubens Right *Adoration of the Mystic Lamb* by the van Eyck brothers

Belgian Artists

Jan van Eyck
The sheer technical brilliance and almost photographic detail of work by Jan van Eyck (c.1390–1441) are self-evident in paintings such as *Virgin and Child with Canon van der Paele (see p25)* and *The Adoration of the Mystic Lamb (see pp26–7)*. Van Eyck's work had a major impact on Italian art, and helped fuel the Renaissance.

Rogier van der Weyden
One of the leading Flemish "Primitives", Rogier van der Weyden (c.1400–64) is best known for the intense emotion of his work, such as *The Seven Sacraments* in the Koninklijk Museum voor Schone Kunsten, Antwerp *(see p103)*. Working mainly in Brussels, he became the leading painter after the death of van Eyck.

Laurent Froimont by Rogier van der Weyden

Hans Memling
German-born Hans Memling (c.1433–94) was probably trained by Rogier van der Weyden, and went on to become one of the most successful artists of his day. His control of composition, colour and detail results in works that combine beauty with profound compassion *(see pp24–5)*.

Pieter Brueghel the Elder
During the 16th century, Flemish artists turned to Italy for inspiration, which muddied their distinctive north European vision. But Pieter Brueghel (c.1525–69) rejected this trend and painted in a personal style based on what he saw around him. His depictions of rural villages have an affectionate charm and honest naivety.

Pieter Paul Rubens
Almost all the best Flemish artists trained in Italy in the 16th century, and no one made more of this experience than Pieter Paul Rubens (1577–1640). He combined his prodigious Flemish technique with Italian flourish to produce art full of verve and dynamism.

Antoon van Dyck
A colleague and friend of Rubens, Antoon van Dyck (1599–1641) matched many of Rubens' skills, and addressed a similar range of subject matter. Van Dyck however, is best known for his portraits. He became court painter to Charles I of England, who rewarded him with a knighthood.

Pieta by Antoon van Dyck

Jacob Jordaens
After Rubens' death, another of his collaborators Jacob Jordaens (1593–1678) became Antwerp's leading painter. He is best remembered for allegorical paintings expressing the *joie-de-vivre* of the Baroque age.

James Ensor
The work of James Ensor (1860–1949) has earned him a reputation as one of art history's great eccentrics. His paintings incorporate skeletons, masks and hideous caricatures *(see p13)*.

Paul Delvaux
Some memorable images of Surrealism came from the studio of Paul Delvaux (1897–1994). He is famous for his sensual, trance-like pictures of somnolent nudes in incongruous settings.

René Magritte
The dreamlike paintings of René Magritte (1898–1967) rank alongside Salvador Dali's work as archetypal Surrealism. The Magritte Museum *(see p14)* displays paintings by the artist, plus photographs, drawings and archives.

Top 10 Lesser-known Belgian Artists

1 Constantin Meunier
Sculptor and painter (1831–1905) known for bronzes of factory workers *(see p79)*.

2 Théo van Rysselberghe
Painter (1862–1926) who used Pointillism to develop a polished and distinctive style.

3 Émile Claus
Post-Impressionist painter (1849–1924) famous for rural scenes of sparkling clarity, achieved through a technique that he called "Luminism".

4 Jean Delville
One of the most inventive of the Symbolists (1867–1953), famed for brilliantly coloured visions of Satanic forces.

5 Léon Frédéric
A Symbolist (1856–1940) whose works combine social realism with poetic vision.

6 Fernand Khnopff
A painter (1858–1928) whose enigmatic Symbolist work is suffused with suppressed sexuality.

7 Léon Spilliaert
A Symbolist (1881–1946) of great originality, whose works, often black and white, are instantly recognizable.

8 Rik Wouters
A painter and sculptor (1882–1916) whose work is full of light, verve and charm.

9 Constant Permeke
A painter (1886–1952) of the second phase of the Sint-Martens-Latem school *(see pp14–15)*, his work has a social edge and dark, gritty textures.

10 Panamarenko
True to Surrealist traditions, this artist (born 1940) creates machines, such as space ships, and stages clearly doomed attempts to make them work.

For the best art galleries **See pp34–5**

Left **Musée Charlier** Right **Musée des Instruments de Musique**

Museums

Musées Royaux d'Art et d'Histoire, Brussels
Belgium's collection of historic national and international treasures is housed in this palatial building. It includes an impressive array of medieval church treasures (in the Salle aux Trésors), tapestries, Art Nouveau sculpture and jewellery, antique costumes and archaeological finds. One of three museums in the Parc du Cinquantenaire *(see p77)*.

Musée des Instruments de Musique, Brussels
Since moving to its new home in a classic Art Nouveau department store, perched on a ridge over-looking the city, "Le MIM" has become one of Brussels' must-see sights. The multifarious exhibits are enhanced by the pleasure of hearing their sounds through headphones *(see pp16–17)*.

Musée Royal de l'Armée et d'Histoire Militaire

Musée Horta, Brussels
The full artistic potential of Art Nouveau is apparent in this museum – formerly the house and offices of Victor Horta, the father of Art Nouveau architecture *(see pp18–19)*.

Musée Charlier, Brussels
A rare opportunity to see inside one of Brussels' *maisons de maître* (mansions). As well as a fine collection of antique furniture, the Hôtel Charlier contains many reminders of its days as a meeting place for the avant-garde set in the early 20th century *(see p68)*.

Gruuthusemuseum, Bruges
For over 100 years this historic house has served as a museum presenting an ever-growing collection of artifacts from daily life – both lowly and grand – dating from Bruges' medieval Golden Age to the 19th century. The exhibits have benefited from a remodelling of the museum *(see p86)*.

Museum voor Volkskunde, Bruges
See life as it was lived by the ordinary folk of Bruges in the often threadbare 19th and early 20th centuries. Fascinating collections of household items, as well as some complete workshops, bring home the extraordinary changes of the last century and a half *(see p89)*.

The Cinquantenaire

The era of great international fairs was launched by the Great Exhibition in Hyde Park, London, in 1851. King Léopold II decided to mount a similar exhibition to mark the 50th anniversary (cinquantenaire) of the founding of Belgium in 1880. The site chosen was marshland to the east of the historic centre of Brussels. A pair of exhibition complexes, linked by a monumental semi-circular colonnade, was commissioned from Gédéon Bordiau. The project was not completed in time for the 1880 jubilee, but building continued and the site

Brabant Raising the National Flag – the symbolic bronze sculpture crowning the central arch of the Palais du Cinquantenaire.

was used for subsequent fairs. The central triumphal arch – topped by a quadriga reminiscent of Berlin's Brandenburg Gate – was completed in 1905 to mark Belgium's 75th anniversary. Bordiau's barrel-vaulted exhibition hall houses the Musée Royal de l'Armée et d'Histoire Militaire. Its twin to the south was destroyed by fire in 1946; its replacement now forms part of the Musées Royaux d'Art et d'Histoire. The Parc and Palais du Cinquantenaire also contain Autoworld (see p77), as well as two curiosities: the Atelier de Moulage (see p41) and the Pavillon Horta (see p45).

7 Design Museum Gent, Ghent

Anyone interested in antique furniture and the history of the decorative arts will love this delightful museum, which follows changing styles from the domestic elegance of the 17th century to the jocular irreverence of Milanese Post-Modernism *(see p96)*.

8 Het Huis van Alijn, Ghent

This evocative folk museum, set out in almshouses founded by the Alijn family in the 14th century, has become a major repository for a huge range of artifacts that were part and parcel of the lives of ordinary Flanders people in past centuries *(see p96)*.

9 Museum Plantin-Moretus, Antwerp

Within a century of Gutenberg's breakthrough in European printing by means of movable type, this 16th-century printing house had become a leader of the publishing revolution. Among the presses and engraving plates, it's still possible to detect the ferment of ideas, and the possibilities of the spread of knowledge, that printing promised *(see p104)*.

10 Museum Mayer van den Bergh, Antwerp

A rich collection of paintings, *objets d'art* and antiques – the product of the drive and wealth of Fritz Mayer van den Bergh *(see p105)*.

Design Museum, Ghent

For unusual museums See pp40–41

Left **Musée Royale de l'Afrique Centrale** Right **Musée de Tram Bruxellois**

🔟 Unusual Museums

1 Centre Belge de la Bande Dessinée, Brussels

As the Belgian Centre of the Comic Strip is the first to admit, comic strips were not invented in Belgium, but the nation has certainly taken them to its heart, and produced a string of gifted artist-writers, the most famous being Hergé, creator of Tintin. The museum is in an Art Nouveau building by Horta (see pp20–1).

2 Musée du Jouet, Brussels

Teddy bears, dolls, miniature farmyards, rocking horses – this toy museum is an Aladdin's cave of delights with exhibits from the 1850s to the present (see p70).

3 Musée Wiertz, Brussels

The studio of the 19th-century painter Antoine Wiertz reveals him as an artist of great self-delusion. Offended by rejection in Paris, he wanted to see Brussels usurp Paris as the capital of Europe. The fact that the European Parliament building is on his doorstep seems spookily visionary (see p79).

The Overhasty Burial by Antoine Wiertz

4 Musée des Égouts, Brussels

Brussels' sewer museum gives an insight into the massive public works that made the city safe to live in during the late 19th century. Visits to a small portion of the vast network by guided tour only.
⊗ *Pavillon de l'Octroi, Porte d'Anderlecht • Map A3 • 02 500 7031 • Open 10am–5pm Tue–Fri (guided tours Thu & Fri) • Adm charge*

5 Musée du Tram Bruxellois, Brussels

With dozens of trams, ancient and modern, lining the silent platforms of an old tram depot, a visit to this museum is a bit like wandering into one of Delvaux's Surrealist paintings. It has far more appeal than its subject matter may suggest (see p78).

6 ModeMuseum (MoMu), Antwerp

"You are what you wear" is the philosophy behind this museum in Antwerp's fashion district. The collection presents the theory and practice of fashion, from 16th-century lace-making to today's cutting-edge Belgian designers, through imaginative displays.
⊗ *Nationalestraat 28 • Map T2 • 03 470 27 70 • www.momu.be • Open 10am–6pm Tue–Sun, 10am–9pm Thu • Admission charge*

7 Béguinage d'Anderlecht, Brussels

Many of these pious settlements for single women still survive *(see p86)*. This small one serves as a museum evoking their lives. Unforgettable charm *(see p80)*.

Béguinage d'Anderlecht

8 Koninklijk Museum voor Midden-Africa (KMMA), Brussels (Tervuren)

The bold scale of this museum almost matches Belgium's ambitions as a colonial power in the Congo, which is the main focus. It is fascinating on several levels: ethnographic, historical and sociological *(see p78)*.

9 Arentshuis (Brangwyn-museum), Bruges

The story of this museum centres on one of those awkward legacies: the gift to Bruges by the British artist Frank Brangwyn (1867–1956) of a large collection of his own paintings and prints. Fortunately, the result is both unusual and rewarding, as he had a highly distinctive eye and was a brilliant draughtsman *(see p87)*.

10 Bijlokemuseum, Ghent

Housed in an old convent, the Bijlokemuseum is a splendidly idiosyncratic collection of historic artifacts, delivering a surprise at every turn *(see p96)*.

Top 10 Unusual Museum Collections

1 Musée Boyadjian du Coeur
The heart as symbol – a heart surgeon's collection of artifacts. ◈ *1, 2, 3: Musées Royaux d'Art et d'Histoire, Brussels (see p77)*

2 La Salle aux Trésors
Fabulous medieval treasures, spectacularly lit.

3 La Salle Wolfers
Valuable collection of Art Nouveau artifacts.

4 Atelier de Moulage
Workshop producing plaster-cast copies of classic sculptures. ◈ *Parc du Cinquantenaire, Brussels (see p77)*

5 The Mannekin-Pis Costume Collection
A selection of the 815 costumes created for the little statue. ◈ *Maison du Roi, Brussels (see p8)*

6 Dinosaur Skeletons
The famous Iguanodons of Bernissart. ◈ *Musée des Sciences Naturelles, Brussels (see p80)*

7 Books Censored by the Inquisition
"Heretical" books ruthlessly swathed in black ink. ◈ *Maison d'Erasme, Brussels (see p80)*

8 Ex Voto Offerings
Tiny models of animals and body parts once used to plead for heavenly intercession. ◈ *Béguinage d'Anderlecht (see p80)*

9 Historic Rubbish
Display showing the archaeological value of waste. ◈ *Archeologisch Museum, Bruges. Mariastraat 36a • Map K5 • Open 9:30am–12:30pm, 1:30–5pm Tue–Sun • Adm charge*

10 Identity Tags for Abandoned Babies
Tragic mementos of mothers and children. ◈ *Maagdenhuis, Antwerp (see p106)*

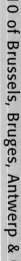

Left **Onze-Lieve-Vrouwekathedraal, Antwerp** Right **Église Notre-Dame du Sablon, Brussels**

Churches

1 Cathédrale des Saints Michel et Gudule, Brussels
Brussels' honey-coloured Gothic cathedral is a sanctuary of calm after the bustle of the Grand Place. Used for royal weddings and funerals (see p68).

2 Église Saint-Jacques-sur-Coudenberg, Brussels
One of Brussels' most distinctive churches occupies a prominent position overlooking the Place Royale: its bell-tower apart, it looks more like a Roman temple than a Christian church (see p68).

3 Église Notre-Dame du Sablon, Brussels
The 15th-century church of the Guild of Crossbowmen is a beautiful example of Brabantine Gothic style, lit by large expanses of stained glass (see p69).

Église Saint-Jean-Baptiste-au-Béguinage

4 Église Saint-Jean-Baptiste au Béguinage, Brussels
The exuberant Flemish Baroque façade of this church contrasts with its history as the focal point of a *béguine* community of women. Something of their charity and moderation still pervades the interior (see p69).

5 Onze-Lieve-Vrouwekerk, Bruges
Bruges' most striking church, with a rocket-like spire in the austere style of Scheldt Gothic. The interior has been tinkered with ceaselessly since the 13th century. Its outstanding treasure is Michelangelo's *Madonna and Child*, donated by a wealthy merchant in 1514 (see p86).

6 Sint-Salvatorskathedraal, Bruges
Both grand and sombre, the tone of this church befits its status as Bruges' cathedral. Although mainly Gothic, Saint Saviour's may date back in origin to early Christian times. The turreted tower was built in Neo-Medieval style in the late 19th century (see p88).

7 Sint-Baafskathedraal, Ghent
Its soaring Gothic interior and Baroque choir give Ghent's impressive cathedral a forceful quality (see p95). It is upstaged, however, by its greatest treasure: Jan and Hubrecht van Eyck's magnificent *Adoration of the Mystic Lamb* (see pp26–7).

Top 10 of Brussels, Bruges, Antwerp & Ghent

At most churches, admission charges apply only to their museums or special exhibits.

Sint-Niklaaskerk

8 Sint-Niklaaskerk, Ghent

The interior of Ghent's most attractive and imposing church has been scrubbed clean by a programme of restoration, resulting in a light and joyous space that makes the most of the robust Gothic stonework *(see p95)*.

9 Onze-Lieve-Vrouwekathedraal, Antwerp

With only one of its two towers finished, Antwerp's cathedral bears the battle scars of its centuries-long struggle for completion, but the immense interior gives a clear indication of the scale of its creators' ambitions. It also provides an apt setting for two stunning triptychs by Rubens, as well as some ravishing late-19th-century paintings *(see pp28–9)*.

10 Sint-Jacobskerk, Antwerp

The richly ornate interior of this church bears testimony to the fact that it was frequented by the well-to-do during Antwerp's 17th-century heyday – among them, Rubens, who was buried in his family chapel here *(see pp104–5)*.

Top 10 Architectural Styles

1 Romanesque

10th–12th centuries. Semi-circular arches and hefty columns. The style is called "Norman" in Britain.

2 Gothic

13th–16th centuries. Pointed arches allowed for lighter structures.

3 Scheldt (or Scaldian) Gothic

13th–14th centuries. An early, rather austere version of Gothic typical of northern Belgium (around the River Scheldt).

4 Brabantine and Flamboyant Gothic

14th–15th centuries. A daintier form of Gothic, used for town halls like Bruges' Stadhuis.

5 Renaissance

15th–17th centuries. An elegant style taking its inspiration from Greek and Roman architecture.

6 Baroque

17th–18th centuries. A lavish interpretation of Classical style, full of exuberance and swagger.

7 Neo-Classical

18th–19th centuries. Classical revisited again, even more determined to emulate Greek and Roman temples.

8 Neo-Gothic

19th-century. Gothic style revisited. Adopted particularly by the Catholic Revival.

9 Art Nouveau

Late 19th–early 20th centuries. A florid, organic style, an effort to create an utterly new approach: hence "new art."

10 Art Deco

1920s–1930s. A brash, angular but glamorous style. Name is based on a decorative arts exhibition in Paris in 1925.

Left **Musée Horta, detail of the ironwork bannisters** Right **Musée des Instruments de Musique**

🔟 Art Nouveau Buildings in Brussels

1 Musée Horta
The home and studio of the great maestro of Art Nouveau architecture, Victor Horta, serves as a master-class in the form *(see pp18–19)*.

2 Hôtel Tassel
Designed by Victor Horta in 1893–5, this is considered the first Art Nouveau house. Up to this point, the well-to-do who commissioned new private mansions in the mushrooming Belgian suburbs adopted any style going: Moorish, Medieval, Tuscan, whatever. Horta extrapolated from this "eclectic" style to evolve something more integrated and considered. The private mansion of a bachelor engineer, Hôtel Tassel was carefully tailored to all aspects of his lifestyle, but this individualized approach also made it less adaptable for subsequent owners. ◈ *Rue Paul-Émile Janson 6, 1050 BRU (Ixelles)*

3 Maison de Paul Cauchie
Behind a façade combining geometric shapes with dreamy Art Nouveau murals lies the home of little-known painter Paul Cauchie (1875–1952). ◈ *Rue des Francs 5, 1040 BRU (Etterbeek) • 02 673 15 06 • Open 1st weekend of every month, 11am–1pm, 2–6pm • Adm charge*

4 Hôtel Saint-Cyr
Art Nouveau tended toward excess, and this accusation might certainly be levelled at this house – all loops and curves, with a circular picture window on the top floor. It was designed for painter Saint-Cyr in 1900. ◈ *Square Ambiorix 11, 1000 BRU (Brussels)*

5 Hôtel Hannon
Swathes of Art Nouveau mansions were cleared from Brussels when the style fell from favour. Hôtel Hannon, built in 1902, is a rarity because some of the internal decorations have survived – and also because the public can gain access to the interior. ◈ *Ave de la Jonction 1, 1060 BRU (Saint-Gilles) • Map G2 • 02 538 42 20 • Open 11am–6pm Wed–Fri, 1–6pm Sat & Sun • Adm charge*

6 Hôtel Ciamberlani
The artist Albert Ciamberlani (1864–1956) was one of those responsible for the huge mural in the triumphal colonnade of the Cinquantenaire building *(see p39)*. He employed Paul Hankar (1859–1901), a key Art Nouveau architect, to build his house and studio in 1897. The façade combines iron, stone and brick for a highly individual decorative effect. ◈ *Rue Defacqz 48, 1050 BRU (Ixelles)*

Hôtel Hannon

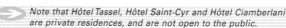

Note that Hôtel Tassel, Hôtel Saint-Cyr and Hôtel Ciamberlani are private residences, and are not open to the public.

7 Musée des Instruments de Musique, Brussels

Art Nouveau was also called "Style Liberty", after the famous London store. Brussels' "Old England" store was named to echo this vogue. The building now houses the Museum of Musical Instruments (see pp16–17).

8 Centre Belge de la Bande Dessinée

Victor Horta designed the Magasins Wauquez, a textile shop, in 1903. Rescued in the 1970s, it has found new life as the famous comic-strip museum (see pp20–21).

Centre Belge de la Bande Dessinée

9 Le Falstaff

Le Falstaff, a famous restaurant and drinking palace opposite the Bourse in the heart of Brussels, dates from 1903, and still powerfully evokes the era in which it was created. The interior is rich in Art Nouveau detail, seen in the stained glass, the mirrors, the lamp fittings and the furniture.

10 De Ultieme Hallucinatie

"Ultimate Hallucination" might be a good description of some of the more extravagant examples of Art Nouveau design. The dining room of this celebrated establishment offers a rare opportunity to eat in an authentic Art Nouveau setting (see p81).

Top 10 Architectural Wonders

1 Jeruzalemkerk, Bruges
A Byzantine-influenced church inspired by a pilgrimage to the Holy Land (see p89).

2 Palais de Justice, Brussels
Joseph Poelaert threw every Neo-Classical style in the book at this vast and domineering monument to justice (see p70).

3 Pavillon Chinois, Tour Japonaise, Brussels
Two beautiful oriental buildings rise up incongruously from the Parc de Laeken (see p77).

4 Serres Royales, Brussels
Architecturally magnificent royal greenhouses built in the 1870s (see p80).

5 Cinquantenaire Arch
A staggering 45-m (147-ft) high Neo-Classical arch with a huge quadriga on top (see p39).

6 Hôtel Saint-Cyr, Brussels
Brussels' weirdest Art Nouveau building (see opposite).

7 Centraal Station, Antwerp
Louis Delacenserie's station is a delicious pot-pourri of Neo-Classical styles (see p106).

8 Palais Stoclet, Brussels
This private mansion, designed by Josef Hofmann and decorated by Gustav Klimt, was the architectural shocker of its day (see p80).

9 The Atomium, Brussels
A giant model of an atom, created for the 1958 Universal Exposition (see p77).

10 Basilique Nationale du Sacré-Coeur, Brussels
There is something strangely soulless about this massive 20th-century church (see p80).

For specialist Art Nouveau tours in Brussels, ask at the tourist office **See p112**

Left **Counts Egmont and Hoorn, Place du Petit Sablon, Brussels** Right **The Revolution of 1830**

Moments in Belgian History

1 50s BC: Julius Caesar

The Roman army suffered repeated setbacks in its struggle against the courageous "Belgae", but in the end Rome won out, and Belgium flourished under the Pax Romana of provincial rule for 400 years.

2 AD 843: Treaty of Verdun

After the Romans came the Franks, whose empire reached its apogee under Charlemagne. After his death, his homeland was split by treaty along the River Scheldt – the division from which Flanders and Wallonia would evolve.

3 1302: Battle of the Golden Spurs

France dominated Flanders for much of the medieval period, eventually resulting in popular revolt. At the Battle of the Golden Spurs, a Flemish rebel force humiliated the cream of the French army.

Philip the Good after Rogier van der Weyden

4 1384: Burgundy takes over

When Louis de Male, Count of Flanders, died in 1384, his title was inherited by his son-in-law Philip the Bold (1342–1404), Duke of Burgundy. The powerful dukes of Burgundy gradually extended their control over the Low Countries. Burgundian rule reached a Golden Age under Philip the Good (reigned 1419–67). Bruges, his capital, was the centre of a rich trading empire.

5 1568: Religious strife

Charles V, Holy Roman Emperor and King of Spain, inherited the Burgundian territories, but faced violent opposition there as Protestantism gathered pace. A decisive moment came in 1568, during the reign of Philip II, when Counts Egmont and Hoorn were executed in the Grand Place for opposing the persecution of Protestants. Eventually the territory was divided into Protestant north (the Netherlands) and Catholic south (now Belgium).

6 1815: Battle of Waterloo

When the Spanish Netherlands passed to Austria in 1713, conservative groups began to agitate for Belgian independence. Their revolt was swept aside in 1794 when the French revolutionary armies invaded. The Belgians were divided over the merits of Napoleonic rule, and fought on both sides when Napoleon was finally defeated by the Allies at Waterloo *(see p62)*.

7 1830: The Belgian Revolution

After Waterloo, the Congress of Vienna placed Belgium under Dutch rule, a deeply unpopular solution. Anger boiled over in 1830, independence was declared, and the Dutch army was forced out of Brussels.

8 1914–18: World War I

At the outbreak of World War I, the German army swept into neutral Belgium. The Belgians thwarted their advance by flooding the land. The front settled near the medieval town of Ypres *(see p63)*. Over the next four years, half a million people from both sides died there.

The Front Line at Ypres, World War I

9 1940–44: World War II

History was repeated in May 1940, when the German army launched a *Blitzkrieg* against neutral Belgium to outflank the Maginot Line, which blocked their entry into France. Brussels was liberated in September 1944.

10 1957: Treaty of Rome

Having been unwitting victims of two World Wars, the Belgians were enthusiastic supporters of the Treaty of Rome, which laid the foundations for the European Union. Over time, Brussels has effectively become the "Capital of Europe".

Top 10 Historical Figures

1 Baldwin Iron-Arm
Baldwin (d. 878) became the first Count of Flanders, making Bruges his stronghold.

2 Pieter de Coninck and Jan Breydel
De Coninck, a weaver, and Breydel, a butcher, led the Flemish rebellion against the French, launched in 1302.

3 Philip the Bold
Philip the Bold ushered in the Burgundian era in the Netherlands after inheriting control of Brussels and Flanders.

4 Philip the Good
Philip the Good (reigned 1419–67) founded the Order of the Golden Fleece and was a great patron of the arts.

5 Charles V
Born in Ghent, Charles V (1500–58) forged the largest empire in Europe since Roman times. His press is mixed.

6 Isabella and Albert
The dazzling court of the Infanta Isabella (1566–1633) and Archduke Albert (1559–1621) marked calmer times for Spanish Habsburg rule.

7 Charles of Lorraine
Austrian governor-general (ruled 1744–80) credited with bringing the Age of Enlightenment to Brussels.

8 King Léopold I
First king of Belgium (ruled 1831–65), popular for his total commitment to the task.

9 King Léopold II
Second king of Belgium (ruled 1865–1909) *(see p78)*.

10 Paul-Henri Spaak
Socialist prime minister during the post-war years, Spaak (1899–1972) played a central role in the creation of the European Community.

For the best exposition of the historical evolution of Brussels, visit the Maison du Roi **See p8**

Left **Hergé** Right **Johnny Hallyday**

TOP 10 Famous Belgians

1 Gerard Mercator

Most school maps of the world are still based on the "Mercator projection" – an ingenious way of representing the spherical globe on a flat page. Mercator (1512–94) is also credited with creating the first "atlas", a word he introduced.

2 Georges Simenon

One of the world's best-selling authors, Simenon (1903–89) was born and bred in Liège. His most famous creation, Inspector Maigret, appeared in 75 of his 400 novels.

Queen Astrid

3 Queen Astrid

Prince Léopold of Belgium married the beautiful Swedish princess Astrid in 1926. By the time of their coronation in 1934, they had three young children, but tragedy struck the following year when she was killed in a car accident in Switzerland, aged 29.

4 Hergé

Georges Remi (1907–83) was a self-taught illustrator from the Brussels suburb of Etterbeek. In 1929 he published a story called *Tintin au Pays des Soviets*, and Belgium's most celebrated comic-strip character was born. Since then, 200 million Tintin books have been sold worldwide in some 50 languages. Georges Remi devised his pen name, Hergé, by simply reversing his initials and spelling out the sounds.

5 Jacques Brel

Jacques Brel (1929–78) still ranks in many people's minds as the greatest singer-songwriter in the French language. Although he first made his name in France, he remained loyal to his Belgian origins. The Jacques Brel Foundation in Brussels celebrates his life and work. ❧ *Place de la Vieille Halle aux Blés 11 • Map C3 • 02 511 10 2 • www.jacquesbrel.be • Open 10:30am–6pm Tue–Sat; last entry 5pm (8pm Thu). Closed Mon & public holidays • Adm charg*

6 Johnny Hallyday

Although Johnny Hallyday (born 1943) is most famous as the "godfather of French rock 'n' roll", Belgium also claims him: his father was Belgian. In a long career he has sold over 100 million records. He has had a parallel career in film acting, impressing critics with his superb performance in the title role of *L'Homme du Train* (*The Man on the Train*, 2003).

 For more on Hergé and Tintin **See pp20–21**

cques Brel

Eddie Merckx

Cycling is big in Belgium, nd no name ranks higher than ddie Merckx (born 1945), five mes winner of the Tour de rance (1969–72 and 1974).

Jean-Claude Van Damme

A former karate champion, ean-Claude Van Damme (born 960) did odd jobs in California, uch as delivering pizzas and ying carpets, before making s name with action thrillers ke *Cyborg*, *Kickboxer* (1989) nd *Universal Soldier* (1992).

Justine Henin-Hardenne

Together with Kim Clijsters *ee below*), Justine Henin has rought Belgian tennis to a new vel. She scored her first Grand lam victory in the French Open 2003, going on to win the US pen later the same year – each me in finals against Clijsters.

Kim Clijsters

Kim Clijsters' father, Lei, set s daughter on an early road to uccess when he built her a clay nnis court at their home in ree, in the eastern province of mburg. In 2003, Clijsters ecame the first Belgian to reach umber one in world rankings.

Top 10 Slightly Less Famous Belgians

1 Andreas Vesalius
Known as "the father of modern anatomy", Vesalius (1514–64) was physician to Charles V and Philip II of Spain.

2 Adolphe Sax
Best known as inventor of the saxophone, Sax (1814–94) devised a range of innovative musical instruments.

3 Father Damien
A missionary (1840–89) who devoted his life to caring for lepers in Hawaii. He was canonised in 2009 by Pope Benedict XVI.

4 Victor Horta
The innovative Art Nouveau architect credited with bringing the style to maturity *(see pp18–19)*.

5 Léo-Hendrik Baekeland
A chemist (1863–1944) who invented Bakelite, the first totally synthetic plastic.

6 Henri van de Velde
Leading Art Nouveau designer (1863–1957) whose work laid the foundations for the Bauhaus movement.

7 Adrien de Gerlache
Pioneer polar explorer (1866–1934) who led the first expedition to overwinter in Antarctica in 1897–99.

8 Jacky Ickx
One of the great Formula One racing drivers of the 1960s and 1970s (born 1945).

9 Anne Teresa De Keersmaeker
A leading choreographer (born 1960) in the world of contemporary dance.

10 Dries van Noten
A celebrated fashion designer (born 1958) who has helped bring Antwerp to the forefront of *haute couture*.

Left **Ommegang, Brussels** Right **Procession of the Holy Blood, Bruges**

🔟 Festivals and Events

1 Ommegang, Brussels
In Brussels' most spectacular parade, some 2,000 participants, dressed as Renaissance nobles, guildsmen, mounted soldiers and entertainers, perform an *ommegang* (tour) in the Grand Place. It's a tradition said to date back to 1549. ⊗ *First Tue & Thu in July*

Planting of the may tree, Brussels

2 Plantation du Meiboom, Brussels
A jolly slice of ancient folklore dating back to 1213. Led by the Confrérie des Compagnons de Saint-Laurent, dressed in wacky costumes, and accompanied by seven traditional giant figures, the participants parade a may tree around central Brussels, before planting it on the corner of the Rue du Marais and Rue des Sables. ⊗ *9 Aug (2pm onwards)*

3 Foire du Midi, Brussels
This big, rollicking, noisy late-summer fun fair set out along the Boulevard du Midi has the newest rides plus dodgems, roller coasters and all the other old favourites. ⊗ *Mid-Jul to mid-Aug*

4 Heilig Bloedprocessie, Bruges
Bruges' biggest day out, the Procession of the Holy Blood follows an 800-year-old tradition 40 days after Easter, the sacred relic of the Holy Blood is paraded around the streets in a colourful spectacular, but at heart solemn procession featuring sumptuous medieval and biblical costumes. ⊗ *Ascension Day (May)*

5 Praalstoet van de Gouden Boom, Bruges
First performed in 1958, the Pageant of the Golden Tree takes place in Bruges every five years or so. In a vast costumed parade the people of the city evoke the glory days of the Burgundian era. ⊗ *Late Aug (next in 2012)*

6 Reiefeest, Bruges
Bruges' river is the Reie. This festival, held every three years, celebrates its role in the city's history. A series of historical scenes is performed at night at various points beside the water creating a magical effect and bringing the city's architecture to life. ⊗ *Last 10 days of Aug (next in 2011)*

7 Gentse Floraliën, Ghent
Every five years, this vast flower show takes place in the Flanders Expo trade fair complex to the south-west of the city centre. Ghent's flower-growing industry is famous above all for its begonias, azaleas, rhododendrons and roses. ⊗ *Late Apr (next in 2010)*

Festival van Vlaanderen
An impressive programme of classical music – as well as jazz, world music and dance – takes place across Flanders every summer and autumn, with performances in the main venues, as well as in churches and other historic buildings. ⌘ www.festival-van-vlaanderen.be • Jun–Oct

Toussaint, all Belgium
All Saints' Day is followed by le Jour des Morts, the Day of the Dead – a time when Belgians honour their departed by tidying up the graveyards and filling them with flowers – over 50 million, apparently, mainly chrysanthemums, which glow softly with autumnal colours. ⌘ 1–2 Nov

Fête de Saint-Nicolas, all Belgium
The Feast of St Nicholas (Sinterklaas in Dutch) is celebrated by children with even greater enthusiasm than Christmas. St Nicholas (the original Santa Claus), dressed as the Bishop of Myra, walks the streets with his blacked-up sidekick Zwarte Piet, and children receive presents, as well as sweets and *speculoos* biscuits. ⌘ 6 Dec

Feast of St Nicholas

Top 10 Spectator Sports and Venues

1 Ronde van Vlaanderen
Classic of the cycling calendar. ⌘ First Sun in Apr

2 Liège-Bastogne-Liège
Oldest cycling classic in the World Cup. ⌘ Third Sun in Apr

3 Zesdaagse van Gent
One of the most important meetings for European speed cycling. ⌘ 't Kuipke, Citadelpark, Ghent • Map P6 • Late Nov

4 Ivo Van Damme Memorial Meeting
The most important athletics meeting in the Belgian sports calendar. ⌘ Stade Roi Baudouin, Brussels • Map F1 • End Aug

5 Brussels 20K Race
Brussels' mini-marathon. ⌘ Last Sun in May

6 Proximus Diamond Games
Prestigious women's tennis international. ⌘ Sportpaleis, Antwerp • Feb

7 Belgian Derby, Ostend
Horsey highlight. ⌘ Wellington Renbaan • Middle Sat in Jun

8 Stade Roi Baudouin
Athletics, cycle meetings and international soccer matches. ⌘ Ave du Marathon 135, 1020 BRU (Laeken) • Map F1 • 02 479 36 54

9 Stade Constant Vanden Stock, Brussels
The home ground of RSC Anderlecht. ⌘ Avenue Théo Verbeeck, 1070 BRU (Anderlecht) • Map F2 • 02 522 15 39 • www.rsca.be

10 Jan Breydel Stadium (Olympiapark), Bruges
Stadium shared by Club Brugge and Cercle Brugge. ⌘ Leopold II-laan, 8200 Bruges (Sint-Andries) • 050 40 21 21 • www.clubbrugge.be

Left **Canal boat trip** Right **Musée du Jouet**

Children's Attractions

Bruparck, Brussels
Near the Atomium *(see p77)* is an amusement designed to entertain all the family – with a multi-screen cinema, swimming-pool complex, bars and restaurants, and a "Mini-Europe" of scale models *(see p80)*.

Mini-Europe and the Atomium

Centre Belge de la Bande Dessinée, Brussels
Older children will be intrigued by this unusual, somewhat specialist museum; younger children may not be, especially if they speak neither French nor Dutch *(see pp20–21)*.

Historic Tram Ride, Brussels
This should appeal to children of all ages. A vintage tram strains and squeaks its way along the wooded path from the Musée du Tram Bruxellois to the Musée Royale de l'Afrique Centrale *(see p78)* and back.

Musée du Jouet, Brussels
Toy museums have a habit of boring children stiff, but this one bucks the trend with its welcoming atmosphere and hands-on exhibits *(see p70)*.

Manneken-Pis Costume Collection, Brussels
You may be lucky to find the Mannekin-Pis *(see p10)* on one of his dressed-up days. In any case it's always fun to see his extra-ordinary wardrobe in the Maison du Roi *(see p8)*, where about 10 of his 815 outfits are on display.

Walibi Belgium
Belgium's premier amuse-ment park, with everything from scary roller coasters and vertical drops to soak-to-the-skin water rides, plus more gentle, traditional tracked car-rides and roundabout for younger visitors. There is also a multi-pool swimming complex called Aqualibi, with a host of shoots and tube-runs. ◎ *Wavre* • *Walibi Belgium: 010 42 15 00. Aqualibi: 010 42 16 03* • *Open Apr–mid-Jul: 10am–6pm daily; mid-Jul–Aug: 10am–8pm daily; Sep–Oct: 10am–6pm Sat–Sun only* • *www.walibi.be* • *Adm charge*

Canal Boat Trips, Bruges and Ghent
From a seat in a canal tour boat, the landmarks of Bruges and Ghent show themselves in a new light. Boats leave from various places in the centre of Bruges *(see p84)* and from the Graslei and Korenlei in Ghent *(see p95)*.

Belfort, Bruges
A kind of medieval theme-ark experience: the physical challenge of a slightly scary spiral staircase, magnificent views from the top, and the therapeutic shock of colossal noise if the bells ring while you are up there. There may even be a queue to get in *(see p85)*.

Boudewijn Seapark, Bruges
Bruges' amusement park, in a suburb to the south of the city centre. Many of the rides and attractions are marine-themed, many designed for younger children. There's also a covered dolphinarium, where dolphins and seals perform. ◈ *Al fons De Baecke-straat 12, 8200 Sint Michiels (Bruges)* • *050 38 38 38* • *www.boudewijnseapark. e* • *Phone for adm times* • *Adm charge (children under 1m tall free)*

Antwerp Zoo
One of the oldest zoos in the world (1843). Special attractions include a sea lion show, elephant bathing, a hippo pond and a hands-on reptile experience. The zoo is also a Centre for Research and Conservation. ◈ *Koningin stridsplein 26* • *Map V2* • *03 202 45 40* • *www.zooantwerpen.be* • *Open 10am–late afternoon daily (closing times vary seasonally between 4:45 & 7pm)* • *Adm charge*

enguins in Antwerp Zoo

Top 10 Other Sights for Children

Parc du Cinquantenaire, Brussels
The three major museums in this park have enough variety to appeal to all ages *(see p77)*.

MIM, Brussels
Music in the headphones changes as you go around – a winning formula *(see pp16–17)*.

Scientastic, Brussels
Fascinating exhibition explains principles of science. ◈ *Bourse Metro Station (level -1)* • *Map B3* • *02 732 13 36*

Musée de Sciences Naturelles, Brussels
Good for the budding scientist, ecologist and dinosaur fanatic *(see p80)*.

Musée des Égouts, Brussels
Underground sewer visits – perennially appealing *(see p40)*.

Musée du Cacao et du Chocolat, Brussels
See, and taste, chocolate in the making. ◈ *Rue de la Tête d'Or 9–11* • *Map C3* • *02 514 20 48*

Musée des Enfants, Brussels
Popular museum for children aged 4–12. Limited numbers. ◈ *Rue du Bourgmestre 15, 1050 BRU (Ixelles)* • *02 640 01 07*

Het Huis van Alijn, Ghent
Magical folk museum *(see p96)*.

Het Gravensteen, Ghent
Heavily restored medieval castle, complete with dungeon. ◈ *Sint-Veerleplein* • *Map P1* • *09 225 93 06*

Nationaal Scheepvaartmuseum, Antwerp
Maritime museum, with real boats to climb on *(see p103)*.

Left **Seletion of bottled beers** Right **Belgian chocolates**

🔟 Things to Buy

1 Chocolate
Belgian chocolate is justly famous. The manufacturers use high-quality cocoa beans and re-introduce a generous proportion of cocoa butter. They also invented the means to manufacture filled chocolates (or pralines) on an industrial scale. As a result, these superb chocolates are remarkably good value.

Lace-making

2 Lace
There were tens of thousands of lace-makers in 19th-century Belgium, many of them living in penury. That industry was under-mined by the invention of lace-making machines, and to some degree it still is. If you want to buy proper, hand-made Belgian lace, go to a reputable shop, insist on a label of authenticity, and expect to pay a high price.

3 Beer
In 1900 there were over 3,200 breweries in Belgium; now there are just over 100, but they still generate an astonishing variety of beers *(see pp58–9)*. The most famous are produced by the Trappist monasteries, but even the lighter, lager-style beer such as Stella Artois and Jupiler are made to a high standard.

4 Biscuits and Pâtisserie
It is hard not to drool in fron of the ravishing shop windows o Belgian pâtisseries – and the mouth-watering offerings taste as good as they look. An alternative is to buy some of the equall famed biscuits (cookies) – from specialist like Dandoy *(see p11)*.

5 Tapestry
Tapestry was one of the great medieval industries of Brussels and Bruges. It is still made on a craft basis, but of course large pieces come at luxury prices.

6 Haute Couture
Over the last two decades, Belgium – Antwerp in particular has shot to the forefront of the fashion world, with designers such as Ann Demeulemeester, Dries van Noten, Raf Simons and Walter Van Bierendonck. Many o the major designers have their own shops in Antwerp *(see p107)* but there are plenty of outlets elsewhere, notably in the Rue Dansaert in Brussels *(see p71)*.

7 Children's Clothes
There are numerous shops devoted to children's clothes in Belgium, and their products are irresistible – from hard-wearing romp-around cottons to beautifully made winter jackets and hats, and fun shoes.

8 Diamonds
Over three-quarters of the world's uncut diamonds flow through the exchanges of Antwerp; many of these are cut, polished and mounted there. You could find some bargains – but of course, you have to know what you're doing. If in doubt, consult the Hoge Raad voor Diamant (HRD), which oversees a reliable system of certification. ❧ *HRD: www.hrd.be*

9 Antiques and Bric-à-brac
For lovers of everything from old comics and Art Nouveau door handles to exquisite Louis XVI desks and ormolu clocks, Belgium is a happy hunting ground. In Brussels, the full range is on view between the Place du Jeu de Balle and the Place du Grand Sablon *(see p71)*.

10 Tintin Merchandise
Tintin fans can pick up not only the books, but also T-shirts, figurines, games, postcards, mobile phone covers, key rings, stationery, mugs – you name it. The characters are copyright, so high-quality, legally produced goods come at a fairly steep price. There are Tintin Shops in central Brussels, Antwerp and Bruges.

Tintin figure

Top 10 Suppliers of Chocolates, Biscuits and Pâtisserie

1 Leonidas
One of the nation's favourite chocolatiers. Less rich and less expensive than its rivals in the top league. ❧ *www.leonidas.com*

2 Godiva
Maker of luxury chocs, with branches worldwide. ❧ *www.godiva.be*

3 Neuhaus
Credited with inventing the praline and the *ballotin* (box). ❧ *www.neuhaus.be*

4 Corné Toison d'Or
Fine chocolates, with a national presence and a shop in the Galeries Royales de St-Hubert in Brussels *(see p10)*.

5 Wittamer
Chocolates, cakes and biscuits to die for *(see p72)*. ❧ *www.wittamer.com*

6 Pierre Marcolini
Fabulous chocolates, made entirely from raw ingredients. ❧ *www.marcolini.be*

7 Mary
Chocolates of exquisite quality. ❧ *www.marychoc.com*

8 Galler
A mass-market but high-standard manufacturer. Its famous *Langues de Chat* (cat's tongues) are shaped in a jokey cat's face.

9 Biscuiterie Dandoy
Supreme biscuit manufacturer, in a class of its own *(see p11)*.

10 Jules Destrooper
Mass market manufacturer of biscuits since 1886. Its distinctive blue-and-white boxes contain such refined delights as "almond thins". ❧ *www.destrooper.com*

Left **Moules-marinières** Right **Waffles**

🔟 Culinary Highlights

1 Frites
Belgian *frites* (fries) are, quite simply, the best in the world. They are deep-fried in good-quality oil not once but twice, so they end up golden brown and *bien croustillantes* (crisp). *Frites* can be a side-dish or – served with a dollop of mayonnaise – a meal in themselves.

Frites frietjes with mayonnaise

2 Shellfish and Crustaceans
Seafood plays a major role in Belgian cuisine. Mussels-and-chips (*moules-frites*) is virtually the national dish. Oysters (raw) and scallops (cooked) are also popular. A favourite lunchtime entertainment is to pick one's way through a *plateau de fruits de mer* (seafood platter).

3 Fish
The North Sea ports are the base for active fishing fleets, which bring in daily catches of sole, skate, sea bass, cod and hake. To see the sheer variety of the catch, visit the Vismarkt (fish market) in central Bruges. Place Sainte-Catherine in Brussels is a centre for fish restaurants.

4 Steak
It may be a standard dish of any restaurant or bistro, but *steak-frites* (steak and chips/fries) can be excellent – just what you need on a cold night. You will understand why the meat is good when you visit a butcher's shop: standards are high, because Belgian customers are knowledgeable and demanding.

5 Filet Américain
Belgians have enough confidence in their beef to eat it raw – as *Filet Américain*. A *toast cannibale* is a snack form of this.

6 Game
Belgian food pays heed to the seasons. Winter is the time for warming game recipes, such as the classic dish *faisan à la brabançonne*, pheasant cooked with caramelized endives. Rabbit, hare, venison, wild boar, pigeon, duck and guinea fowl are also much cherished. Much of the "game" is now farm-raised.

Chicons au gratin (Belgian endive)

Cooking with Beer

Several of Belgium's classic dishes are cooked with beer – notably the beef stews called *carbonnades flamandes* or *Vlaamse stoverij*. In some restaurants (such as Den Dyver in Bruges, see p92), almost the entire menu involves beer.

Belgian Endive

A great Belgian invention. When trying to overwinter *chicorée* lettuce in around 1840, a Brussels gardener found it produced succulent, salad-like shoots. They can be eaten raw, but their sweet, slightly bitter flavour really emerges when they're cooked, either as a vegetable accompaniment or in dishes such as *chicons au gratin*. Chicon is the French word, *witloof* the Dutch; in English, it's endive or chicory (but it's confusing, as these terms can also refer to lettuce).

Pâtisserie

Every village and community in Belgium has a good pâtisserie; most shopping streets have several. These supreme concoctions of fresh fruit, chocolate, cream, *crème pâtissière*

Profiterole

and, of course, pastry, are an integral part of Belgian life.

Waffles

Waffles (*gaufres/wafels*) are a great Belgian tradition. Freshly made and sprinkled with icing sugar, they are eaten as a snack at fun fairs, at the seaside, in shopping streets. They are associated with celebrations, and families will get out their own waffle-irons on festive occasions.

Top 10 Classic Belgian Dishes

1 Carbonnades Flamandes/Vlaamse Stoverij
A beef stew cooked in Belgian beer – rich, succulent and sweet, and best eaten with *frites*, mustard and mayonnaise.

2 Moules-marinière
Mussels steamed, until they open, in white wine flavoured with celery, onion and parsley; usually served in something resembling a bucket, accompanied by a plate of *frites*.

3 Waterzooi
A creamy, comforting dish of chicken (or fish) in broth; a traditional dish of Ghent.

4 Chicons au Gratin
Belgian endives wrapped in ham and baked in a creamy cheese sauce.

5 Anguilles au Vert/ Paling in 't Groen
Eels cooked in a sauce of fresh green herbs.

6 Garnaalkroketten
Deep-fried potato croquettes filled with fresh shrimps; an excellent starter or snack.

7 Salade Liégeoise
A warm salad of potatoes and green beans, or *salade frisée*, with fried bacon bits.

8 Stoemp
Mashed potato mixed with a vegetable, such as carrots or celeriac, or a meat purée.

9 Flamiche aux Poireaux
A quiche-like tart, made with leeks.

10 Jets d'Houblon
Hop-shoots – a spring-time by-product of brewing, usually served in a cream sauce. They taste a bit like asparagus.

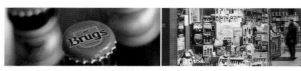

Left **Brugs Witbier bottles** Right **Specialist beer shop**

🔟 Types of Belgian Beer

1 Trappist Beer
In the past, some of Belgium's finest beers were made by the Trappists, a silent order of Cistercian monks. Now it's produced commercially by five breweries with close ties to the monasteries (Chimay, Westmalle, Orval, Rochefort and Westvleteren). Yeast is added at bottling to induce a second fermentation, so pour off carefully in one go to avoid disturbing the sediment.

Chimay

2 Abbey Beer
Other abbeys also produced beer, but unlike the Trappist monasteries, many have licensed them to commercial breweries. Leffe, for example, is now closely connected with InBev. That said, many of the abbey beers are excellent. In addition, there are good "abbey-style" beers, such as Ename, Floreffe and St Feuillien.

3 Witbier/Bière Blanche
Most beer is made from barley, but it can also be made from wheat to produce a distinctive "white beer" to which flavourings such as coriander and orange peel may be added. The result is a light, sparkling and refreshing beer, often served cloudy with sediment. Examples: Hoegaarden, Brugs Tarwebier.

4 Lambic
In the valley of the Senne, the river that flows through Brussels, there is a natural airborne yeast called *Brettanomyces*. For centuries, brewers have simply left their warm wheat-beer wort uncovered during the winter months, and allowed air to deliver the yeast into it. The fermenting beer is then left to mature in wooden casks for a year or more. This creates a very distinctive beer, with a slightly winey edge, called *lambic* – the quintessential beer of Brussels.

5 Gueuze
Lambic of various ages can be blended, and then fermented a second time in the bottle. This produces a beer called *gueuze*, fizzy like champagne and matured a further year or two to accentuate the winey qualities of the original product.

6 Kriek
Lambic can be flavoured with cherries (formerly the cherries of the north Brussels orchards of Schaerbeek), added during fermentation to create a highly distinctive drink called *kriek*; with raspberries, to make *framboise*; or with candy sugar, to make *faro*. Of the three, newcomers may find *faro* the easiest to begin with.

Kriek

There are specialist beer bars in all the main cities, serving hundreds of kinds of beer.

Double/Triple

Traditionally, breweries graded their beers by strength: apparently single was around 3%, double 6% and treble 9%. Some breweries – notably the Abbeys – still label their beers double (dubbel) and triple (tripel). Double is usually a dark and sweetish brew, triple often golden-blond.

Brugse Tripel

Lager-style Beers

Lager, or *pils*, is a bottom-fermented beer: the yeast remains at the bottom of the brew (stronger, heavier ales tend to be top-fermented, which seals in more flavour). Although such light beers may be sniffed at by connoisseurs abroad, in Belgium they are brewed to a high standard. Despite its ubiquity, InBev's famous Stella Artois, brewed at Leuven, is a good-quality lager.

Strong Ales

Some breweries pride themselves on the sheer power of their product. Duvel ("Devil"), at 8.5%, is a famous example. Several lay claim to being the strongest beer in Belgium; at 12%, Bush beer is up there, and to be treated with respect.

Duvel

Christmas Beers

Many of the breweries produce Christmas ales for the festive season. These may just be prettily labelled versions of their usual brew, but may also be enriched ales of high strength.

Top 10 Beer Places

1 Musée Bruxellois de la Gueuze, Brussels
Probably the best brewery museum in Brussels, at the quaint old Cantillon brewery *(see p80)*.

2 A la Mort Subite, Brussels
A famous café-bar in central Brussels, with a *gueuze* named after it *(see p72)*.

3 Chez Moeder Lambic, Brussels
A justly revered beer-shrine in Saint-Gilles, which serves 450 kinds of beer *(see p81)*.

4 In 't Spinnekopke, Brussels
A famous old *estaminet* (traditional pub), serving a range of dishes cooked with beer *(see p75)*.

5 Huisbrouwerij De Halve Maan, Bruges
A small, visitable brewery – producers of Straffe Hendrik ("Strong Henry") *(see p88)*.

6 't Brugs Beertje, Bruges
A classic beer pub, offering some 300 kinds of beer, including a range of "guest beers" on tap *(see p91)*.

7 Den Dyver, Bruges
A restaurant specializing in beer cuisine, served with fine beers *(see p92)*.

8 In de Plantenmarkt, Bruges
Popular with locals, this pub serves a good selection of beers *(see p91)*.

9 Dulle Griet, Ghent
A celebrated pub serving 250 brands of beer *(see p98)*.

10 Kulminator, Antwerp
A specialist beer bar with 500 brands, including what is claimed to be the world's strongest beer.

 Specialist beer shops sell the full range, and many of the top brands are also available from supermarkets.

Left **Le Botanique, Brussels** Right **De Vlaamse Opera, Ghent**

🔟 Performing Arts Venues

1 Théâtre Royal de la Monnaie, Brussels

The most revered performing arts venue in the country, La Monnaie (Dutch: De Munt) is celebrated for sparking off the Revolution of 1830 *(see p47)*, when a crowd took to the streets incited by Auber's opera *La Muette de Portici*. It was rebuilt in elegant Neo-Classical style in 1819; the interior was redesigned following a fire in 1855. La Monnaie has highly respected opera and ballet companies. ✆ *Place de la Monnaie • Map C2 • 070 23 39 39 • www.lamonnaie.be*

2 Palais des Beaux-Arts, Brussels (BOZAR)

Victor Horta's Palais des Beaux-Arts was completed in 1928. Know as BOZAR, it is a multi-arts venue, covering music, theatre, art, dance and much more. ✆ *Rue Ravenstein 23 • Map D4 • 02 507 82 00 • www.bozar.be*

3 Le Botanique, Brussels

The beautiful glasshouses of Brussels' botanical gardens were built in 1826–9. Cunning conversion of the interior has provided what is now a key venue for a wide range of cultural activities, including theatre, dance and concerts of all kinds. ✆ *Rue Royale 236, 1210 BRU (Saint-Josse-ten-Noode) • Map D1 • 02 218 37 32 • www.botanique.be*

4 Conservatoire Royal de Musique, Brussels

The Brussels conservatory is a highly respected institution. Its buildings, completed in 1875, were designed by the architect of the Galeries Royales de Saint-Hubert *(see p10)*, and include a classical music venue. ✆ *Rue de la Régence 30 • Map C5 • 02 500 87 17/8*

5 Les Halles de Schaerbeek, Brussels

The magnificent old covered market, built in iron and glass at the end of the 19th century, has been transformed into an inspirational venue for a variety of cultural events – including drama, dance and music. ✆ *Rue Royale Sainte-Marie 22b, 1030 BRU (Schaerbeek) • Map G2 • 02 218 21 07 • www.halles.be*

6 Théâtre Royal de Toone, Brussels

The Toone marionette theatre, occupying a tiny building at the bottom of a medieval alley, is a Brussels institution. Note this is not for children: the plays – enacted by traditional puppets made of wood and papier-mâché – may be serious classics of theatre, and the language is often Bruxellois, the rich dialect of the city. ✆ *Petite Rue des Bouchers 21 (Impasse Schuddeveld 6) • Map C3 • 02 513 54 86 • www.toone.be*

Théâtre Royal de Toone

7 Concertgebouw, Bruges

As part of its celebrations as a Cultural Capital of Europe in 2002, Bruges undertook to create a new concert hall. The result is a highly innovative building that has quickly become established as a leading venue for classical music, as well as ballet and jazz. ✆ *'t Zand 34 • Map J5 • 070 22 33 02 • www.concertgebouw.be*

8 De Vlaamse Opera, Ghent

Ghent home of the much-respected Vlaamse Opera, this classic opera house ranks among the most spectacular theatres in Europe. ✆ *Schouwburgstraat 3 • Map Q3 • 09 268 10 11 • www.vlaamseopera.be*

De Vlaamse Opera, Antwerp

9 De Vlaamse Opera, Antwerp

Antwerp's opera house was completed in 1907, its interior elegantly decked out with marble and gilding. The Vlaamse Opera performs here and in Ghent. ✆ *Van Ertbornstraat 8 • Map U2 • 03 202 10 11 • www.vlaamseopera.be*

10 deSingel, Antwerp

This vibrant multi-purpose cultural centre is a venue for performances and exhibitions of drama, dance, architecture and music. ✆ *Desguinlei 25 • 03 248 28 28 • www.desingel.be*

Top 10 Belgian Writers, Poets and Musicians

1 Roland de Lassus
Also known as Orlando di Lasso (c.1532–94). One of the leading composers of his day.

2 César Franck
Organist and composer (1822–90) in the Romantic tradition.

3 Émile Verhaeren
Symbolist poet (1855–1916) noted for his portrayals (in French) of Flanders.

4 Maurice Maeterlinck
Nobel-Prize-winning Symbolist poet and dramatist (1862–1949).

5 Michel de Ghelderode
Belgium's most celebrated 20th-century playwright (1898–1962), and one of the most original writers in the French language.

6 Georges Simenon
Prolific master of the popular detective story (1903–89) and creator of Inspector Maigret *(see p48)*.

7 Django Reinhardt
The most celebrated of all jazz guitarists, Reinhardt (1910–53) was a key member of the renowned Quintet of the Hot Club of France.

8 Arthur Grumiaux
A leading violinist of his era (1921–86).

9 Hugo Claus
Belgium's most revered writer (1929–2008), a Bruges-born poet, playwright and novelist.

10 Amélie Nothomb
One of Belgium's most successful modern novelists (born 1967), noted for her exploration of the darker sides of human nature.

Left **Butte de Lion, Waterloo** Right **Forêt de Soignes**

🔟 Excursions

Waterloo
Among the fields and farm-houses near Waterloo, 15 km (9 miles) south of Brussels, Napoleon was finally defeated. The battlefield has been a tourist site virtually since the battle itself. The modern Visitor Centre, next to the Butte de Lion mound, is a useful place to start. ⚅ *Route du Lion 252–4, 1420 Braine-l'Alleud • Open daily Apr–Sep: 9:30am–6:30pm; Oct–Mar: 10:30am–5pm • Adm charge*

Walibi Belgium
Belgium's biggest and best-known theme park – a good day out for the kids *(see p52)*.

Forêt de Soignes
The magnificent ancient beech forests of Soignes provide a splendid landscape for walking or cycling – particularly in autumn, when the beech trees turn golden. There are two arboretums, at Groenendaal and Tervuren, and an information centre on the site of the 14th-century Abbaye de Rouge-Cloître. ⚅ *Drève du Rouge-Cloître 4 • 02 660 64 17*

Namur

Namur
An attractive town on the confluence of the Rivers Meuse and Sambre, Namur is famous above all for its mighty Citadelle (open Jun–Sep), perched dramatically on a steep-sided hill. ⚅ *Tourist Office: Square Léopold • 081 24 64 49 • www.pays-de-namur.be*

Leuven
The old university town of Leuven (French: Louvain) has a deep charm, derived from its compact human scale and many historic buildings – chief among them the Stadhuis, the most beautiful Gothic town hall of them all. ⚅ *Tourist Office: Naamsestraat 1 • 016 20 30 20 • www.leuven.be*

Mechelen
Mechelen (French: Malines) was a proud trading city in the Burgundian era, and centre of power under Margaret of Austria (1507–30). Dominating the city is the vast bell-tower of the fine Gothic Sint-Romboutskathedraal – originally intended to be twice as high. ⚅ *Tourist Office: Hallestraat 2–4 • 070 22 28 00 • www.mechelen.be*

Ostend
Ostend (spelt Oostende locally) is famous as a resort and for its excellent seafood. It also has surprisingly good collections of art, in the Provinciaal Museum voor Moderne Kunst and the Museum voor Schone Kunsten. ⚅ *Tourist Office: Monacoplein 2 • 059 70 11 99 • www.toerisme-oostende.be*

Waterloo, Six Flags Belgium, the Fôret de Soignes, Namur, Leuven, Mechelen and Lier can all be easily reached from Brussels.

Lier

8 This pretty little town to the south-east of Antwerp has a handsome collection of historic buildings clustered around the Grote Markt, but its most famous possession is the Zimmertoren, a 14th-century watch-tower with the fascinating Centenary Clock on its façade. ◈ *Tourist Office: Grote Markt 57 • 038 00 05 55 • www.lier.be*

In Flanders Fields, Ypres

Damme

9 A pretty cluster of late-medieval buildings is all that remains of the once-prosperous town at the head of the canal to Bruges. A pleasant excursion by bus or bicycle. ◈ *Tourist Office: Huyse de Grote Sterre, Jacob van Maerlantstraat • 050 28 86 10 • www.damme-online.com*

Ieper (Ypres)

10 Ieper (French: Ypres) was one of the great medieval trading cities of Flanders. Its historic past was all but erased when it became the focal point of bitter trench warfare in World War I. Today it is the centre for visits to the trenches and the

Centenary Clock, Lier

many cemeteries, and site of the Menin Gate, the memorial arch marking the road along which so many soldiers marched, never to return. But the real draw is "In Flanders Fields", a superb museum depicting the background and course of the war, its experiences, textures and horrors – a richly informative and deeply moving experience. ◈ *In Flanders Fields: Lakenhallen, Grote Markt 34 • 057 23 92 20 • www.ieper.be; www.inflandersfields.be • Open Apr–18 Nov: 10am–6pm daily; 19 Nov–Mar: 10am–5pm Tue–Sun. Closed 3 weeks in Jan • Adm charge*

Ostend and Damme are short journeys from Bruges. Ieper (Ypres) is most conveniently visited from Bruges or Ghent.

AROUND BRUSSELS, BRUGES, ANTWERP & GHENT

TOP 10 OF BRUSSELS, BRUGES, ANTWERP & GHENT

Left **Place du Petit Sablon** Right **Grand Place**

Central Brussels

THE CENTRE OF BRUSSELS IS NEATLY CONTAINED *within a clearly defined shape called the Pentagon. Nowadays this outline is formed by a busy ring road called the Petite Ceinture. The road follows the path of the old city walls, a huge 14th-century construction 9 km (6 miles) long. Few traces of the walls have survived, but one old city gate, the Porte de Hal, still stands, and gives a fair indication of just how massive the fortifications must have been. Most of historic Brussels is contained within these bounds, including both the commercial and popular districts of the Lower Town, and the aristocratic quarter of the Upper Town, which includes the Royal Palace. The result is that Brussels is still a very compact city. You can walk right across the Pentagon in about half an hour. As well as monuments and cultural gems, you will find a concentration of excellent places to stay and eat, good shops, and vibrant cafés and bars.*

Tintin and Snowy

Sights

1 Grand Place

2 Musées Royaux des Beaux-Arts

3 Musée des Instruments de Musique

4 Centre Belge de la Bande Dessinée

5 Manneken-Pis

6 Cathédrale des Saints Michel et Gudule

7 Musée Charlier

8 Église Saint-Jacques-sur-Coudenberg

9 Sablon

10 Église Saint-Jean-Baptiste au Béguinage

Preceding pages **Brabo Fountain, Grote Markt, Antwerp**

Grand Place
No trip to Brussels would be complete without a visit to the Grand Place – even if it's just to stock up on some Belgian biscuits or chocolates. A remarkable legacy of the city's Gothic and Renaissance past, it is also a monument to the values and ingenuity of the artisans and merchants who were the architects of Brussels' prosperity (see pp8–9).

Musées Royaux des Beaux-Arts
This is a superb, "must-see" collection, notable because it focuses almost exclusively on Flemish and Belgian art. Highlights include rare works by Pieter Brueghel the Elder, the exhilarating Rubens collection, and an unparalleled assembly of works by the Belgian Symbolists, as well as the Magritte Museum showcasing an extensive collection (see pp12–15).

Musée des Instruments de Musique
The famous "MIM" collection of historical and contemporary musical instruments is housed in

Manneken-Pis

the remarkable Art Nouveau department store known as "Old England". Take the children too: easy-to-use infrared headphones bring the exhibits to life by showing visitors what the instruments sound like when played (see pp16–17).

Centre Belge de la Bande Dessinée
Reflecting the huge popularity of comic-strip books in Belgium – and, indeed, most of continental Europe – this unique "Belgian Centre of the Comic Strip" is a shrine to the art form. Archive material and other exhibits focus above all on Belgian contributors to the genre – most notably, of course, on Hergé, the creator of Tintin (see pp20–21).

Manneken-Pis
In Brussels you can't avoid this cheeky little chap, famously pissing with carefree abandon just as little boys do. Among other things, he's on postcards, T-shirts, key rings and corkscrews. So why not take a pilgrimage to see the real thing – a tiny bronze statue – and bask in the happy absurdity of it all? It must be worth a photograph (see p10).

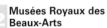

Le Ruisseau by Léon Frédéric, Musées Royaux des Beaux-Arts

For Brussels tourist information See p112

67

6 Cathédrale des Saints Michel et Gudule

Brussels' largest and finest church, built over three centuries from 1225 onward, has been restored. The honey-coloured stone of its 15th-century twin towers glows from the cathedral's raised pedestal, especially in the evening light. It is a fine example of the light and flowery style called Brabantine Gothic. The soaring space of the interior is impressive. It contains some fine 16th-century stained glass and a wonderful Baroque pulpit (1699). Dedicated to St Michael, patron saint of the city, the cathedral's name also

Cathédrale des Saints Michel et Gudule

acknowledges St Gudule, a local 8th-century saint who outfoxed the Devil. ⊗ *Parvis Sainte-Gudule • Map D3 • 02 217 83 45 • Open 7am–6pm Mon–Fri, 8:30am–3:30pm Sat, 2pm–6pm Sun. • Admission charges only for Museum of Church Treasures and Crypt*

7 Musée Charlier

Brussels is a city of grand old 19th-century mansions, or *maisons de maître*. This museum provides a rare opportunity to see inside one. The original owner, Henri van Curtsem, commissioned Victor Horta (see p49) to redesign the interior. In the hands of van Curtsem's adoptive heir, sculptor Guillaume Charlier, the mansion became a centre for Brussels' avant-garde. On his death in 1925, Charlier left the house to the city, and it retains much of the decor of his era. There are works by leading artists of the time, such as James Ensor, Léon Frédéric, Fernand Khnopff and Rik Wouters, plus an impressive collection of antique furniture. ⊗ *Avenue des Arts 16 • Map E3 • 02 220 26 91 • Open noon–5pm Mon–Thu, 10am–1pm Fri • Admission charge*

8 Église Saint-Jacques-sur-Coudenberg

This charming 18th-century church, with its Roman-style façade and lantern bell tower, sits on the top of the Coudenberg, the aristocratic enclave of the Upper Town. It is attached to the Royal Palace, and has seats for the royal family in the choir. During the anticlerical days of the French occupation in the 1790s, it was converted first to a "Temple of Reason" and then a "Temple of Law" before reconsecration in 1802. ⊗ *Place Royale • Map D4 • Open 10am–6pm daily • Free*

The Pentagon

The first city walls to enclose Brussels were built in about 1100 but the city expanded and they were superseded in 1379, creating the neat pentagon shape that is evident today. These walls were eventually knocked down in the mid-19th century to make way for tree-lined boulevards. Of the city gates, only the Porte de Hal remains.

For more Brussels churches See pp42–3

Église Saint-Jacques-sur-Coudenberg

9 Sablon

The name Sablon refers to the sandy marshland that occupied this site until it was reclaimed in the 17th century. The Place du Grand Sablon is a centre for antiques and is home to two of Brussels' leading chocolate makers: Wittamer and Pierre Marcolini. The Place du Petit Sablon is dominated by its park, which is adorned with 48 statues of the medieval guilds of Brussels. Separating the two is the Église Notre-Dame du Sablon.
⊙ Rue de la Regence 3B • Map C4
• Open 8am–6pm daily • Free

10 Église St-Jean-Baptiste au Béguinage

Béguinages were pious institutions for single women (see p86). This one was built in the 17th century. The façade is full of Baroque detail, while inside, the mood is one of calm. Note the tombstones of the béguines set in the floor.
⊙ Place du Béguinage • Map B1
• 02 217 87 42 • Open 10am–5pm Tue–Sat, 10am–8pm Sun • Free

A Day in the Centre

Morning

Start off with the essentials: a stroll around the **Grand Place** (see pp8–9) and a trip to the **Manneken-Pis** (see p10), stopping for a waffle at the Dandoy shop in Rue Charles Buls on the way. Now head back to the Bourse (see p10), and go west along Rue Dansaert, the street for cutting-edge fashion. Turn right at the Rue du Vieux Marché aux Grains and walk up to the **Église Sainte-Catherine**, a church designed in 1854 by Joseph Poelaert, who was also responsible for the colossal Palais de Justice. It stands on reclaimed land at the head of a canal now covered over by the Place Sainte-Catherine. This was the site of the old fish market, and is still famous for its fish restaurants. It could be the place to stop for a spot of lunch.

Afternoon

Walk back east, stopping at the **Cathédrale des Saints Michel et Gudule** before heading up the hill to Rue Royale. Take a stroll in the pleasant **Park de Bruxelles,** then walk south to the **Palais Royal** (see p70) and the elegant 17th-century Place Royale, with its statue of the 11th-century crusader Godefroi de Bouillon. You're now a stone's throw from both the **Musées Royaux des Beaux-Arts** and the **Musée des Instruments de Musique** (see p67). Take your pick. After this, you'll probably need some refreshments, so continue down the Rue de la Régence to the cafés and chocolate shops of the **Sablon** district.

Left **Palais Royal** Right **Église Notre-Dame de la Chapelle**

Best of the Rest

1 Galeries Royales de Saint-Hubert
When it opened in 1847, this elegant shopping arcade was the grandest in Europe *(see p10)*.

2 Musée du Costume et de la Dentelle
Exquisite examples of costume and lace, an industry that employed 10,000 women in mid-19th-century Brussels *(see p10)*.

3 Place des Martyrs
The 445 "martyrs" killed in the Belgian Revolution of 1830 lie buried in this square. ◉ *Map C2*

4 Église Notre-Dame de la Chapelle
This large, atmospheric church is like something out of a Brueghel painting – aptly so, since Pieter Brueghel the Elder is buried here.
◉ *Place de la Chapelle • Map B4 • 02 513 53 48 • Open Jun–Sep: 9am–5pm Mon–Sat, 11:30am– 4:30pm Sun; Oct–May: 12:30–4:30pm daily • Free*

5 Palais Royal and Les Musée Belvue
See how the other half lived in the grand rooms of the Royal Palace, one of whose wings now houses a museum devoted to the history of Belgium since 1830.
◉ *Place des Palais. Map D4 • Palais Royal: 02 551 20 20. Open Jul–Sep: 10:30am–4:30pm Tue-Sun. Free • Musée Belvue: 02 512 2 21. Open Jun–Sep: 10am–6pm Tue–Sun; Oct–May: 10am–5pm • Adm charge*

6 Palais de Charles de Lorraine
This suite of 18th-century rooms contains a small but select exhibition of furniture, porcelain, clock and other artifacts. ◉ *Place du Musée 1 • Map C4 • 02 519 53 11 • Ope 1pm–5pm Sat only • Adm charge*

7 Musée du Cinéma
A fascinating collection, in the foyer of a cinema, tracing th early history of the moving image. ◉ *Rue Baron Horta 9 • Map D4 • 02 551 19 00 • Open daily • Adm charg*

8 Porte de Hal
The sole surviving gate of the 14th-century city walls.
◉ *Boulevard du Midi • Map B6 • 025 34 15 18 • Open 9:30am–5pm Tue–Fri; 10am–5pm Sat & Sun.*

9 Palais de Justice
There is something gloriously megalomaniac about this vast Ne Classical pile. ◉ *Place Poelaert • Ma B5 • 02 508 65 78 • Ope 8am–5pm Mon–Fri • Free*

10 Musée du Joue
This delightful toy museum appeal. to both adults and children alike. ◉ *Rue de l'Association 24 • Map E2 • 02 219 61 68 • Ope 10am–noon & 2–6pm dai • Adm charge*

Left **Galerie Bortier** Right **Galeries Royales de Saint-Hubert**

10 Shopping

Galeries Royales de Saint-Hubert
A spectacularly elegant and spacious shopping arcade built in 1847 (see p10).

Rue Neuve
A pedestrianized shopping street close to the city centre, with many of the main European fashion chains and a large Inno department store at the northern end. ◈ Map C1

Rue Antoine Dansaert
Ignore the shoddy environs: this is the place for cutting-edge fashion. All the Antwerp designers are represented in the shops here, and there are several outlets for notable Belgian fashion labels. ◈ Map B2

Galerie Bortier
This is a small, rather dowdy sister to the Galeries Royales de Saint-Hubert. Here you'll find second-hand books, prints, postcards and posters. ◈ Map C3

Place du Grand Sablon
There are antique shops fronting onto the square, but try looking around in some of the side passages as well. Two of the finest chocolatiers, Wittamer and Marcolini, are here (see p55). ◈ Map C4

Avenue and Galerie Louise
Top-name international couturiers cluster around the Place Louise, while more boutiques lie within a covered arcade that connects the Avenue de la Toison d'Or to the Avenue Louise. ◈ Map C5

Galerie de la Toison d'Or
Another covered arcade of up-market boutiques close to the Porte de Namur. ◈ Map D5

Christmas Market
From early December to early January, this market offers all things Christmassy – crafts, decorations, presents – in the streets to the west of the Grand Place and around the Bourse. ◈ Map B3

Rue Blaes and Place du Jeu de Balle
The Place du Jeu de Balle has a daily flea market (6am–2pm). In recent years, shops selling antiques, junk and curios have spread up the Rue Blaes to the north. ◈ Map B5

Galerie Agora
This maze-like covered arcade sells T-shirts, baseball caps, leather goods, costume jewellery and incense – all surprisingly in the lower price range. ◈ Map C3

Visit the Place du Grand Sablon for the weekend antiques market.

Left **La Chaloupe d'Or** Right **Café du Vaudeville**

TOP 10 Bars and Cafés

Le Roy d'Espagne
A famous watering-hole in the old bakers' guildhouse. There is a medieval air to the interior decor. Also serves light meals. ® *Grand Place 1 • Map C3*

La Chaloupe d'Or
An elegant café and restaurant in the old tailors' guildhouse. A good spot for a light lunch, an afternoon beer or a pâtisserie. ® *Grand Place 24–25 • Map C3*

Café du Vaudeville
Not many cafés can claim to have had Marx, Rodin and Victor Hugo among their clientele, but the Vaudeville has a long history. Sit outside in the city's most splendid arcade, or upstairs in a salon decorated with copies of the Communist Manifesto. ® *Galerie de la Reine 11 • Map C3*

A La Mort Subite
"Sudden Death" may sound alarming, but this famous bar, redesigned in Rococo style in 1926, is named after a dice game. It is also the name of a *gueuze* beer *(see pp58–9)*. ® *Rue Montagne aux Herbes Potagères 7 • Map C2*

Delirium Tremens
With pink elephants dangling from the ceiling, free Wi-Fi and over 2,000 different beers, this bar has made an impact on the Belgian drinking scene. ® *Impasse de la Fidélité 4A • Map C2*

Chez Toone
Hidden away from the tourist throngs, the famous Toone puppet theatre *(see p60)* has an atmospheric bar serving decent beers and light meals. ® *Petite Rue des Bouchers 21 (Impasse Schuddeveld 6) • Map C3*

Greenwich Tavern
An established Brussels favourite, especially popular with an avid chess-playing crowd. It was a former hang-out of Magritte. ® *Rue des Chartreux 7 • Map B2*

Wittamer
The world-class chocolatier has seating where you can sample its heavenly products with a cup of tea or coffee. ® *Place du Grand Sablon 12–13 • Map C4*

MIM
The Musée des Instruments de Musique's spectacular roof-top café *(see pp16–17)*. ® *Rue Montagne de la Cour 2 • Map D4*

Le Corbeau
The house speciality, at this popular under-30s haunt, is the *Chevalier* – a litre of beer that should be downed in one attempt. ® *Rue Saint-Michel 18–20 • Map C1*

Left **The Music Village** Right **L'Archiduc**

10 Brussels Nightlife

1 L'Archiduc
The 1930s Art Deco interior of this elegant bar was designed to evoke a cruise-liner. A grand piano tinkles jazz numbers. ✆ *Rue Antoine Dansaert 6–8 • Map B2*

2 Le Fuse
Behind the gritty industrial exterior lies the best disco in town. World-class DJs spin a mix of techno and drum'n' bass. ✆ *Rue Blaes 208 • Map B5 • 02 511 97 89*

3 Studio Athanor (Blow-up Club)
A popular setting for Saturday nights of house, electro, "NuPunk" and "NuJazz"; jazz and blues on Tuesday nights. ✆ *Rue de la Fourche 17–19 • Map C3 • 02 514 16 15*

4 Le Bazaar
A chic disco offering world music, two bars and a restaurant serving world food, on Fridays and Saturdays. ✆ *Rue des Capucins 63 • Map B5 • 02 511 26 00*

5 The Music Village
A stylish venue with table-seating for food and drink around a stage from 7pm. Jazz on Fridays and Saturdays, rock and blues on Wednesdays and Afro-Latino on Thursdays. ✆ *Rue des Pierres 50 • Map B3 • 02 513 13 45*

6 Recyclart
A multi-purpose "artistic laboratory" in the old Chapelle-Kapellekerk railway station which plays host to a variety of performers and runs weekend club-night events. ✆ *Rue des Ursulines 25 • Map B4 • 02 502 57 34*

7 Mappa Mundo
An atmospheric, cosmopolitan bar in the lively Saint-Géry area that keeps humming into the early hours. ✆ *Rue du Pont de la Carpe 2–6 • Map B3 • 02 513 51 16*

8 Soixante
A popular and lively disco with DJs playing "streaming music" (funk, garage and so on) Wednesdays to Saturdays. ✆ *Rue du Marché au Charbon 60 • Map B3 • 02 514 51 49*

9 Culture Museum
A lively nightspot, a few metres from the Grand Place, with Cuban DJs and an international crowd. ✆ *Rue du Marché aux Fromages 10 • Map C3 • 02 502 76 89*

10 Havana
The ambience may be Latin but the music comes in all varieties at this lively dance club. Open late – all night at weekends. Three bars, restaurant. ✆ *Rue de l'Épée 4 • Map B5 • 02 502 12 24*

Left **La Belga Queen** Right **Kasbah**

Restaurants

Comme Chez Soi
1 Brussels' most celebrated restaurant has two Michelin stars. For a taste of the superlative, innovative French cuisine, be sure to book weeks ahead. ✆ *Place Rouppe 23 • Map B4 • 02 512 29 21 • Closed Sun, Mon • €€€€€*

L'Ecailler du Palais Royal
2 One of Brussels' most prestigious fish restaurants is now under a new team bringing young flair to the range of classic dishes. ✆ *Rue Bodenbroeck 18 • Map C4 • 02 512 87 51 • Closed Sun • €€€€€*

La Belga Queen
3 A stylish but essentially fun new restaurant in an ornate former bank. The French-Belgian menu is good value, particularly at lunchtime. ✆ *Rue du Fossé-aux-Loups 32 • Map C2 • 02 217 21 87 • €€€€*

Chez Marius en Provence
4 Set in an 18th-century house, this restaurant specializes in fish, with Mediterranean touches. ✆ *Place du Petit Sablon 1 • Map C5 • 02 511 12 08 • Closed Sun • €€€€*

Sea Grill, SAS Radisson
5 On offer at this Michelin-starred fish restaurant is serious, refined eating in a Scandinavian-inspired setting. ✆ *Rue du Fossé-aux-Loups 47 • Map C2 • 02 227 31 31 • Closed Sat L, Sun • €€€€€*

La Belle Maraîchère
6 Come here for a classic Brussels experience: top-rate fish cookery in a traditionally-styled, family-run restaurant. It's been a favourite with the locals for three decades. ✆ *Place Sainte-Catherine 11 • Map B2 • 02 512 97 59 • Closed Wed, Thu • €€€€€*

La Marée
7 This small restaurant has a reputation for excellent, simple fish cookery. The emphasis is placed on good food and good value. ✆ *Rue de Flandre 99 • Map B1 • 02 511 00 40 • Closed Mon, Tue • €€*

Kasbah
8 Sample succulent Moroccan dishes in a magical "Arabian Nights" setting beneath scores of coloured lanterns. ✆ *Rue Antoine Dansaert 20 • Map B2 • 02 502 40 26 • €*

Aux Armes de Bruxelles
9 Founded in 1921, Aux Armes de Bruxelles is an institution: white-linen elegance and impeccable Belgian cooking. ✆ *Rue des Bouchers 13 • Map C3 • 02 511 55 50 • Closed Mon • €€€*

Rôtisserie Vincent
10 Dine on robust and well-judged Belgian dishes, in a room decorated with marine murals. Very meaty! ✆ *Rue des Dominicains 8–10 • Map C2 • 02 511 26 07 • €€*

***Note:** Most Brussels residents avoid the tourist restaurants in the Rue des Bouchers.*

Price Categories

For a three-course meal for one with half a bottle of wine (or equivalent meal), taxes and extra charges.

€	under €30
€€	€30–€40
€€€	€40–€50
€€€€	€50–€60
€€€€€	over €60

verne du Passage

10 Lunch Spots, Brasseries & Bistros

1 Brasserie de la Roue d'Or
A popular Art-Nouveau rasserie with Magritte-esque nurals, offering good-value elgian and French cooking. ◎ *ue des Chapeliers 26 • Map C3 • 02 14 25 54 • €€*

2 In 't Spinnekopke
An appealing *estaminet* raditional pub) that stands by its 8th-century heritage to present menu of fine Belgian-Bruxellois ishes. ◎ *Place du Jardin-aux-Fleurs 1 Map A3 • 02 511 86 95 • Closed Sat L, un • €€*

3 L'Entrée des Artistes
This popular and reliable rasserie serves well-judged are, with some good Belgian tandards among them, such as *hicons au gratin.* ◎ *Place du Grand ablon 42 • Map C4 • 02 502 31 61 • €€*

4 Museum Brasserie
This stylish brasserie is arved out of a corner of the 1usées Royaux. If you're feeling dventurous, try the carpaccio of eef or tuna. Good wine list. ◎ *Place Royal 3 • Map 4 • 02 508 35 80 Closed Mon • €€€€*

5 Brasserie Horta
Located in the omic Strip Museum, lorta offers a daily nenu of local dishes. ◎ *Rue des Sables 20 Map D2 • 02 217 72 71 Closed Mon • €€*

6 Le Pain Quotidien
Selling excellent bread with delicious fillings, as well as tempting pastries, Le Pain Quotidien ("Daily Bread") is a runaway success. This is the most central of the 10 city branches. ◎ *Rue Antoine Dansaert 16 • Map B2 • €*

7 Chez Patrick
This cherished and popular restaurant refuses to change or diverge from its traditions of solid, good-value, truly Belgian cooking. ◎ *Rue des Chapeliers 6 • Map C3 • 02 511 98 15 • Closed Sun, Mon • €€*

8 Taverne du Passage
A traditional 1930s Belgian diner with accomplished waiters and an enthusiastic local clientele. The fish dishes are excellent. ◎ *Galerie de la Reine 30 • Map C3 • 02 512 37 31 • Closed Wed, Thu (Jun–Jul) • €€€*

9 't Kelderke
A 17th-century cellar-restaurant delivering feasts of Belgian cuisine. The good food attracts appreciative locals as well as tourists. ◎ *Grand Place 15 • Map C3 • 02 513 73 44 • €*

10 Chez Léon
Established in 1893, this *moules-frites* specialist is now an international brand. ◎ *Rue des Bouchers 18 • Map C3 • 02 513 04 26 • €€*

Left **Autoworld** Right **Musée Royal de l'Armée et d'Histoire Militaire**

Outer Brussels

OVER THE CENTURIES, BRUSSELS EXPANDED *beyond the old city walls, gradually absorbing neighbouring towns and villages. These outlying communes – such as Ixelles, Saint-Gilles and Anderlecht – still retain their distinctive characters. As a result, there is huge variety across Outer Brussels. An excellent public transport system makes it easy to scoot around these suburbs, and the highlights listed here are definitely worth the journey.*

Sights

1. Parc du Cinquantenaire
2. Musée Horta
3. Musée David et Alice van Buuren
4. Pavillon Chinois and Tour Japonaise
5. The Atomium
6. Musée du Tram Bruxellois
7. Musée Royal de l'Afrique Centrale
8. Musée Communal d'Ixelles
9. Musée Constantin Meunier
10. Musée Antoine Wiertz

Tour Japonaise

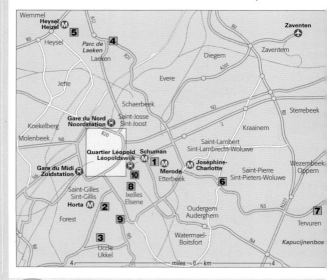

Musée Horta

Parc du Cinquantenaire

In 1880 King Léopold II staged a grand international fair to celebrate the 50th anniversary of the founding of his nation. The vast exhibition halls he erected, together with their successors, now contain a cluster of major museums. By far the most spectacular is the Musées Royaux d'Art et d'Histoire, a rich collection of treasures from around the world, including archaeological finds, anthropological artifacts and decorative arts. Close by are the Musée Royal de l'Armée et d'Histoire Militaire (an extensive military museum) and Autoworld (a major collection of historic cars). The park also contains the extraordinary Atelier de Moulage (see p41), and the Pavillon Horta, a Neo-classical work designed by a young Victor Horta to house erotic sculpture by Jef Lambeaux (1852–1908). ◈ Map H4 • Musées Royaux d'Art et d'Histoire: Parc du Cinquantenaire 10. 02 741 72 11. www.kmkg-mrah.be. Open 9:30am–5pm Tue–Fri, 10am–5pm Sat–Sun. Closed Mon and public hols. Adm charge (free 1–5pm 1st Wed of month) • Musée Royal de l'Armée: Parc du Cinquantenaire 3. 02 737 78 11. www.klm-mra.be. Open 9am–noon, 1–4:45pm. Closed Mon and public hols. Free • Autoworld: Parc du Cinquantenaire 11. 02 736 41 65. www.autoworld.be. Open Apr–Sep: 10am–6pm daily; Oct–Mar: 10am–5pm daily. Adm charge

Musée Horta

A symphony in Art Nouveau design (see pp18–19).

Musée David et Alice van Buuren

This beautifully preserved Art Deco home has excellent furniture and stained glass, as well as contemporary paintings. ◈ Ave Léo Errera 41, 1180 BRU (Uccle) • Map G3 (inset) • 02 343 48 51 • www.museumvanbuuren.com • Museum & garden open 2pm–5:30pm Wed–Mon • Adm charge

Pavillon Chinois and Tour Japonaise

Another legacy of King Léopold, the Chinese Pavilion and Japanese Tower now house porcelain, samurai armour and Art Nouveau stained glass. ◈ Ave Van Praet 44, 1020 BRU (Laeken) • Map G1 • 02 268 16 08 • www.kmkg-mrah.be • Open 9:30am–5pm Mon–Fri, 10am–5pm Sat & Sun • Adm charge

The Atomium

This giant model of a metal molecule was built as Belgium's exhibit at Brussels' 1958 Universal Exposition. ◈ Boulevard du Centenaire, 1020 BRU (Laeken) • Map F1 • 02 475 47 77 • www.atomium.be • Open 10am–6pm daily • Adm charge

The Atomium

Musée du Tram Bruxellois

6 Musée du Tram Bruxellois

The trams of modern Brussels are the last vestiges of a transport system that has formed an integral part of the city's character. Visitors cannot fail to be won over by this extensive collection of over 60 trams, from the horse-drawn "hippomobiles" of the 1860s to sleek expressions of 1960s modernity, all housed in an old tram depot. You can also enjoy a 20-minute ride on a historic tram to (and from) Tervuren (and the Africa Museum) or the Parc Cinquantenaire. ◈ Ave de Tervuren 364B, 1150 BRU (Woluwe-Saint-Pierre) • Map G2 • 02 515 31 08 • www.tram museumbrussels.be • Open 1st weekend Apr–1st weekend Oct: 2–6pm Sat–Sun and public hols • Admission charge (additional charge for ride on historic tram)

7 Koninklijk Museum voor Midden-Africa (KMMA)

The Royal Museum of Central Africa represents a grandiose enterprise: the huge and elegant Neo-Classical palace built in the early 1900s to promote the wonders of Belgium's greatest colonial possession, the vast tract of Central Africa called the Congo. The original purpose – education and glorification – has been sorely compromised by the uncomfortable re-evaluation of Belgium's colonial history in recent years. There are numerous anthropological exhibits, including a vast canoe hewn from a single tree trunk, plus mementos from the history of exploration, such as Henry Stanley's cap. ◈ Leuvensesteenweg 13, 3080 Tervuren • Map H2 • 02 769 52 11 • www. africamuseum.be • Open 10am–5pm Tue–Fri, 10am–6pm Sat–Sun • Admission charge

8 Musée Communal d'Ixelles

It's well worth the trek to this southern suburb for this small but unusually choice municipal art collection. It has a number of minor works by great masters including Rembrandt, Delacroix and Picasso, as well as an excellent collection of posters by Toulouse-Lautrec. This is also a good place to see more work by Symbolists such as Léon Spilliaert and Léon Frédéric, and the much-cherished sculpture and Fauve-style painting of Rik Wouters. ◈ Rue J Van Volsem 71, 1050 BRU (Ixelles) • Map E6 • 02 515 6421 • www.musee-ixelles.be • Open 1–6:30pm Tue–Fri, 10am–5pm Sat–Sun. Closed Mon and public hols • Free (except during exhibitions)

King Léopold II

Belgium's second king reigned from 1865 to 1909, a time of great change in Europe. He was an enthusiast of modernization, and undertook many grand building projects. Determined to make Belgium a colonial power, he created the Belgian Congo. Léopold II cut a distinctive figure with his long, bib-like beard, but his reputation was sullied by well-publicized philandering.

---

9 Musée Constantin Meunier

Constantin Meunier (1831–1905) was one of the great sculptors of the late 19th century, internationally famous for his instantly recognizable bronzes of working people – especially *puddleurs* (forge workers). The museum occupies his former home, and contains excellent examples of his work. ⊗ *Rue de l'Abbaye 59 1050 BRU (Ixelles) • Map G2 • 02 648 44 49 • www.fine-arts-museum.be • Open 10am–noon, 1–5pm Tue–Fri. Closed Mon, weekends and public hols • Free*

Musée Antoine Wiertz

10 Musée Antoine Wiertz

This is one of the most extraordinary museums in Brussels. Antoine Wiertz (1806–65) was an artist whose self-esteem far outstripped his talent. As a young man, he was egged on by patrons, and success went to his head. This grand studio was built so he could paint works on a scale to rival Michelangelo. The grandiose canvases are interesting in themselves, but so too are the smaller works, many so macabre and moralistic they inspire wonderment and mirth. ⊗ *Rue Vautier 62, 1050 BRU (Ixelles) • Map F5 • 02 648 17 18 • www.fine-arts-museum.be • Open 10am–noon, 1–5pm Tue–Sun. Closed Mon, public hols and Sat–Sun in Jul–Aug • Free*

A Walk through the Brussels of Léopold II

Morning

🕐 Put on your best walking shoes, because you're going to cover at least 5 km (3 miles) of pavement and take in half a dozen museums. You don't have to do them all, of course, and don't try this on a Monday, when most of the museums are closed. Start at the Schuman métro station in the heart of the European Quarter, close to the Justus Lipsius Building. If you're feeling energetic, stride up Rue Archimède to admire the weirdest Art Nouveau building of them all – the **Hôtel Saint-Cyr** in Square Ambiorix *(see p44)*. Otherwise, head into the **Parc du Cinquantenaire** *(see p77)* and take your pick of the museums. To refresh yourself, go to **Place Jourdan**, where there are cafés and restaurants to suit all pockets.

Afternoon

Cross the Parc Léopold to visit the wacky **Musée Wiertz** *(see left)*, then walk about 1km (1000 yd) to the delightful **Musée Communal d'Ixelles** *(see opposite)*. If you've had enough already, you could slink into the trendy **Café Belga** in the 1930s Flagey radio building *(see p81)*; otherwise, push on down the Chaussée de Vleurgat to the **Musée Constantin Meunier** *(see above left)*. Now you're only 10 minutes away from the **Musée Horta** *(see pp18–19)*. From here you can get a tram home, or wander around the Art Nouveau houses in the vicinity *(see pp44–5)* and finish the day at the super-trendy **Salons de l'Atalaïde** *(see p81)*.

For more on Belgian artists See pp36–7

Left **Parlement Européen** Right **Maison d'Erasme**

Best of the Rest

1 Musée Bruxellois de la Gueuze

If you visit only one brewery museum, this splendid cobwebby example should be it. ⊗ *Rue Gheude 56, 1070 BRU (Anderlecht)* • *Map A4* • *02 521 49 28* • *www.cantillon.be* • *Open 8:30am–5pm Mon–Fri, 10am–5pm Sat* • *Closed Sun & public hols* • *Adm charge*

2 Maison d'Erasme

This charming red-brick house where Dutch humanist Erasmus stayed in 1521 is now a museum evoking his work. ⊗ *Rue du Chapitre 31, 1070 BRU (Anderlecht)* • *Map F2* • *02 521 13 83* • *Open 10am–6pm Tue–Sun* • *Adm charge*

3 Béguinage d'Anderlecht

Tiny *béguinage (see p86)* – now a museum showing how the *béguines* lived. ⊗ *Rue du Chapelain 8, 1070 BRU* • *Map F2* • *02 521 13 83* • *Open 10am–noon, 2–5pm Tue–Sun* • *Adm charge*

4 Basilique Nationale du Sacré-Coeur

The largest Art Deco building ever built? Remarkable view from its copper-green dome. ⊗ *Parvis de la Basilique 1, 1083 BRU (Ganshoren)* • *Map F2* • *02 425 88 22* • *Open Easter–Oct: 9am–5pm; Nov–Easter: 10am–4pm* • *Free (adm charge for panorama only)*

5 Parlement Européen

The Quartier Léopold is now dominated by the huge glass-and-steel barrel vault of the European Parliament building. ⊗ *Rue Wiertz 43, 1047 BRU* • *Map F5* • *02 284 21 03* • *www.europarl.eu.int* • *Free*

6 Muséum des Sciences Naturelles

See some of the first complete dinosaur skeletons. ⊗ *Rue Vautier 29* • *Map F5* • *02 627 42 38* • *www.sciences naturelles.be* • *Open 9:30am–4:45pm Tue–Fri, 10am–6pm Sat–Sun* • *Adm charge*

7 Serres Royales

Fabulous royal greenhouses. ⊗ *Ave du Parc Royal (Domaine Royal), 1020 BRU* • *Map G1* • *02 513 89 40* • *Open Apr–May* • *Adm charge*

8 Musée René Magritte

Magritte's modest abode. ⊗ *Rue Esseghem 135, 1090 BRU* • *Map F1* • *02 428 26 26* • *www.magrittemuseum.be* • *Open 10am–6pm Wed–Sun* • *Adm charge*

9 Palais Stoclet

Deeply Art Nouveau mansion, built 1905–11. ⊗ *Ave de Tervuren 279, 1150 BRU (Woluwe-Saint-Pierre)* • *Map G2*

10 Bruparck

Family leisure park. ⊗ *Bvd du Centenaire 20, 1020 BRU* • *Map F1* • *02 474 83 77* • *www.bruparck.com* • *Open Apr–Dec: 9:30am–5pm* • *Adm charge*

La Quincaillerie

Price Categories

For a three course meal for one with half a bottle of wine (or equivalent meal), taxes and extra charges.

€	under €30
€€	€30–€40
€€€	€40–€50
€€€€	€50–€60
€€€€€	over €60

🔟 Restaurants, Cafés and Bars

1 Bruneau
One of Brussels' finest. Chef Jean-Pierre Bruneau has earned two Michelin stars. ◈ Ave Broustin 73–5, 1083 BRU (Ganshoren) • Map F2 • 02 421 70 70 • www.bruneau.be • Closed Tue D, Wed • €€€€€

2 La Quincaillerie
A restaurant in a converted hardware store whose spectacular interior put designer Antoine Pinto on the map. ◈ Rue du Page 45, 1050 BRU (Ixelles) • Map G2 • 02 533 98 33 • www.quincaillerie.be • Closed Sat L, Sun L • €€€

3 Les Salons de l'Atalaïde
A truly theatrical restaurant in a grand setting. ◈ Chaussée de Charleroi 89, 1060 BRU (Saint-Gilles) • Map C6 • 02 534 64 56 • €€€

4 La Brouette
Gourmet food in an unpretentious setting. ◈ Boulevard Prince de Liège 61, 1070 BRU (Anderlecht) • Map F2 • 02 522 51 69 • www.labrouette.be • Closed Sat L, Sun D, Mon • €€€

5 Tsampa
Vegetarian restaurant known for its Asian-inspired dishes and happy atmosphere. ◈ Rue de Livourne 109, 1050 BRU (Ixelles) • Map G2 • 02 647 03 67 • Closed Sat & Sun • €

6 De Ultieme Hallucinatie
Sophisticated Art Nouveau restaurant, serving French-Belgian food. ◈ Rue Royale 316, 1210 BRU (Saint-Josse) • Map E1 • 02 217 06 14 • Closed Sat L, Sun, mid-Jul–mid-Aug • €€€

7 La Canne en Ville
A delightful restaurant in a delicately converted butcher's shop. French-based cooking. ◈ Rue de la Réforme 22, 1050 BRU (Ixelles) • Map G2 • 02 347 29 26 • Closed Sat L, Sun & weekends Jul & Aug • €€€

8 Café Belga (Flagey building)
Trendy café that draws a young arty crowd. Small wonder, given its setting in the extraordinary 1930s Art Deco Flagey radio building. Also a thriving music venue. ◈ Place Eugène Flagey • Map G2 • 02 640 35 08 • www.cafebelga.be

9 Chez Moeder Lambic
A welcoming pub devoted to beer, with 450 kinds listed in its menu. ◈ Rue de Savoie 68, 1060 BRU (Saint-Gilles) • Map G2 • 02 539 14 19

🔟 Colmar
An outpost of the Colmar chain in a 16th-century building that was once a Spanish prison. ◈ Boulevard de la Woluwé 71 • Map H2 • 02 762 98 55 • www.colmar.be • €

Left *Portrait of a Bruges Family* by Jacob van Oost (Groeningemuseum) Right **Memlingmuseum**

Bruges

I N THE MIDDLE AGES, BRUGES *was one of Europe's most prosperous cities. Its wealth derived from trade which brought silks, furs, Asian carpets, wine, fruits, even exotic pets to its busy network of canals. Then in about 1500 Bruges fell from grace and slumbered for four centuries. It remained a pocket sized medieval city, its poverty alleviated by almshouses, pious institutions, and a cottage industry supplying Europe's thirst for lace. In the late 19th century, antiquarians recognized Bruges as a historic gem, and began a campaign of preservation and restoration. The city has been a tourist destination since that time, and has recently undergone a second renaissance, with a new generation bringing reinvigorated flair to hotels, restaurants and bars. Bruges has internationally famous collections of art, but is also a wonderfully walkable city, with surprising views on every corner.*

Belfort

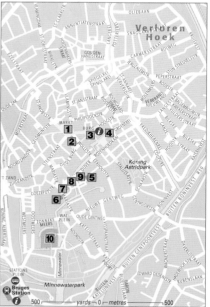

🔟 Sights

1 **Markt**

2 **Belfort**

3 **Burg**

4 **Steenhouwersdijk and Groenerei**

5 **Groeningemuseum**

6 **Memlingmuseum**

7 **Onze-Lieve-Vrouwekerk**

8 **Gruuthusemuseum**

9 **Arentshuis (Brangwynmuseum)**

10 **Begijnhof**

Preceding pages **Waterside building, Bruges**

Markt

The central marketplace of Bruges still retains much of its original outline flanked by old step-gabled guildhouses, but the Provinciaal Hof, the provincial government building on the eastern side, is actually a late-19th-century creation. The Markt remains the focal point of Bruges, and is the site of a large market on Wednesday mornings, and a small Christmas market (with an ice rink) in December. ◈ *Map K4*

Belfort

For a breathtaking view over Bruges' medieval streets, climb the 366 steps to the top of the Belfort (belfry). The set of bells at the top include the 47 carillon bells that are rung by a mechanism installed in 1748. But they can also be played manually from a keyboard on the floor below by the town's *beiaardier* (carillon player) – Bruges' highest paid official, as the joke goes.
◈ *Markt 7 • Map K4 • Open 9:30am–5pm daily (last entry 4:15pm) • Adm charge*

Burg

This intimate and fetching square – a glittering confection of historic architecture, sculpture and gilding – was the focal point of old Bruges *(see pp22–3)*.

Groenerei

Steenhouwersdijk and Groenerei

Just south of the Burg is one of the prettiest stretches of canal, where calm waters reflect the medieval bridges and skyline. Here, the Steenhouwersdijk (stonemason's embankment) becomes the Groenerei (green canal) and is flanked by a picturesque almshouse called De Pelikaan, dated 1714 and named after the symbol of Christian charity, the pelican.
◈ *Map L4*

Groeningemuseum

Not only is this one of the great north European collections, with star roles played by the late medieval masters of Flemish painting, such as Jan van Eyck and Hans Memling; it is also refreshingly small *(see pp24–5)*.

Markt

6 Memlingmuseum and Sint-Janshospitaal

Hans Memling (1435–94) was one of the leading artists of Burgundian Flanders, and the St John's Hospital ranked among his most important patrons. Visitors are advised to use the excellent audioguides available with the entry ticket. The old medieval hospital wards display a fascinating miscellany of treasures, paintings and historic medical equipment; there is also a 15th-century pharmacy. The exhibition culminates in the chapel, which contains the hospital's priceless collection of Memling paintings *(see pp24–5)*.

Onze-Lieve-Vrouwekerk

7 Onze-Lieve-Vrouwekerk

The towering spire of the Church of Our Lady is another key landmark of Bruges' skyline. It's a strange architectural mishmash: the exterior is a good example of the rather austere style known as Scheldt Gothic, and was built over two centuries from 1220 onward. The interior is essentially Gothic, with Baroque flourishes to its statues and extravagant pulpit (1743). This is a rather surprising setting for one of the great treasures of northern Europe: Michelangelo's

Béguinages

A feature of the Low Countries, these communities were founded in the 13th century as sanctuaries for the many women *(béguines)* left single or widowed by the Crusades. Although deeply pious, a *béguinage* or *begijnhof* was not a convent: the *béguines* could leave to marry. Surviving *béguinages* are still used for social housing, with their modest charms intact.

Madonna and Child (1504–5) – a work that came here by virtue of Bruges' close links to Renaissance Italy. The church's museum includes the beautiful gilt-brass tombs, rich in contemporary detail, of Charles the Bold (1433–77), Duke of Burgundy, and his daughter Mary (1457–82). ◐ *Mariastraat • Map K5 • Open 9:30am–4:30pm Mon–Fri, 9:30am–4:40pm Sat, 1:30–4:50pm Sun • Admission charge for museum (church free)*

8 Gruuthusemuseum

If it is hard to picture quite how life was led during Bruges' past, this museum will do much to fill in the gaps. It presents a rich collection of everyday artifacts from the homes of the merchant classes, from kitchenware to musical instruments, furniture, textiles and weapons. The 15th-century building was once the palace of the Lords of Gruuthuse, who became wealthy through a tax on beer flavourings *(gruut)*; as a mark of their status, the house has a gallery overlooking the choir of the Onze-Lieve-Vrouwekerk next door. The house was restored in the 19th century to exhibit the pieces that founded this collection. ◐ *Dijver 17 • Map K4 • Open 9:30am–5pm Tue–Sun • Adm charge (with Archaeological Museum, see p41)*

Arentshuis (Brangwynmuseum)

Frank Brangwyn (1867–1956) was a gifted painter, born in Bruges, the son of William Curtis Brangwyn, one of a group of British artists and architects involved in restoring the city to its Gothic glory. Frank Brangwyn donated an impressive collection of his work to the city. It is now exhibited on the upper floor of the late-18th-century Arentshuis. The ground floor is used for temporary exhibitions. ◈ *Dijver 16* • *Map K4* • *Open 9:30am–5pm Tue–Sat* • *Admission charge*

Begijnhof

This beautiful enclave, home to a community of *béguines* (see box) from 1245 until 1928, expresses something essential about the soul of Bruges. Around the tree-shaded park are the 17th- and 18th-century whitewashed homes of the *béguines*. You can visit the grounds, the *béguinage* church and one of the houses (*Begijnhuisje*). ◈ *Wijngaardstraat* • *Map K5* • *Grounds open during daylight. Begijnhuisje open Mar–Nov: 10am–noon, 1:45–5pm daily; Dec–Feb: 10am–noon Mon, Tue & Fri, 2–4pm Wed–Thu* • *Adm charge to Begijnhuisje (grounds free)*

Begijnhof

A Day In Bruges

Morning

🕤 A day of wandering. Begin in the **Burg** (see pp22–3) and head south across Blinde Ezelstraat. Linger beside the canals on **Steenhouwersdijk** and **Groenerei** (see p85); walk through Huidenvettersplein to the **Dijver** for the prettiest views of the city. Now make your way past **Onze-Lieve-Vrouwekerk** (see opposite) to **Mariastraat** and **Katelijnestraat**, where

☕ you could stop for a divine hot chocolate at **De Proeverie** (see p91). Take Wijngaardstraat to the **Begijnhof** (see left), loop around the **Minnewater** (see p88), and head back along Katelijnestraat. Note the almshouses that pop up in several places on this street (for instance at Nos 87–101 and 79–83).

🍴 For lunch, try the **Vismarkt** area – Wijnbar Est, for example (see p91).

Afternoon

Now you are going to pass through the city's medieval trading centre. From the **Markt** (see p85) walk up Vlamingstraat. At **Beursplein**, there was a cluster of national "lodges" – headquarters of foreign traders – such as the **Genoese Lodge** (No 33). The world's first stock exchange, **Huis ter Beurze**, was at No 35 (see p88). Take Academiestraat to **Spiegelrei** (see p88). Then walk up Langerei to follow the canal that eventually leads to **Damme** (see p63), where goods were transferred from ships to canal barges. Head back down Sint-Jakobstraat, taking a detour to **'t Brugs Beertje** (see p91), with its famed collection of beers.

Left **Minnewater** Right **Diamond Museum**

TOP 10 Best of the Rest

1 Sint-Salvatorskathedraal
It was at St Saviour's that the Order of the Golden Fleece met in 1478. Their coats of arms can be seen in the choir. ◈ *Steenstraat • Map K4 • Open 9–10:15am 2–5:45pm Sat, 2–5pm Sun–Fri • Free*

2 Huisbrouwerij De Halve Maan
Follow the beer-making process at this brewery, in operation since 1856. ◈ *Walplein 26 • Map K5 • 050 33 26 97 • www. halvemaan.be • Tours Apr–Oct: 10am–4pm Mon–Fri, 10am–5pm Sat–Sun; Nov–Mar: 11am–3pm Mon–Fri, 11am–4pm Sat–Sun • Adm charge*

3 Godshuis De Vos
The almshouses *(godshuizen)* of Bruges are easily identified by their humble whitewashed walls, inscribed with names and dates. This delightful example dates from 1643. ◈ *Noordstraat 2–8 • Map K5*

4 Minnewater
Romantic, tree-lined lake formed by a sluice gate on the River Reie – a hectic port in medieval times. ◈ *Map K6*

5 Diamant-museum Brugge
The history of diamonds explained. ◈ *Katelijnestraat 43 • Map K5 • 050 34 20 56 • www.diamondhouse.net • Open 10:30am–5:30pm daily • Adm charge*

6 Sint-Walburgakerk
This handsome Jesuit church, built in 1619–43, is a Baroque symphony in black and white marble, with a supreme wooden pulpit. ◈ *Sint-Maartensplein • Map L3 • Easter–Sep: 8–10pm daily • Free*

7 Huis ter Beurze
This much-restored house – a medieval inn where merchants exchanged credit notes – is the site of the world's first stock exchange. ◈ *Vlamingstraat 35 • Map*

8 Spiegelrei
This beautiful stretch of canal once led into the heart of the city. At Jan van Eyckplein 2 is the Old Toll House; opposite, wealthy merchants met in the Poortersloge. ◈ *Map L3*

9 Sint-Gilliskerk
The pretty parish church of St Giles is unusual for the barrel vault over its nave. Burial place of Hans Memling. ◈ *Map L2 • Open May–Sep: 10am–noon & 2–5pm Mon–Sat, 11am–noon & 2–5pm Sun • Free*

10 Sint-Jakobskerk
The church of St James is Bruges' richest parish church containing notable paintings and tombs. ◈ *Map K3 • Open Jul–Aug only: 2–5:30pm Mon–Fri, Sun, 2–4pm Sat • Free*

Peaceful Minnewater is a popular spot for walkers and picnickers

Left **Kantcentrum** Right **Kruispoort**

10 Eastern Bruges: Sint-Anna

1 Onze-Lieve-Vrouw ter Potterie
This charming little museum combines treasures, oddities and an elaborate Baroque chapel. ❂ *Potterierei 79 • Map L1 • Open 9:30am–12:30pm, 1:30–5pm Tue–Sun • Adm charge*

2 Duinenbrug
Bruges' canals were spanned by little drawbridges to allow boats to pass. This one is a re-construction from 1976. ❂ *Map L2*

3 Museum voor Volkskunde
Occupying almshouses in the east of the city, Bruges' folk museum presents a fascinating collection of historic artifacts. ❂ *Balstraat 43 • Map L3 • Open 9:30am–5pm Tue–Sun • Admission charge*

4 Sint-Annakerk
Elegantly refurbished after destruction by the iconoclasts, this pretty church is a tranquil place of worship enlivened by Baroque flourishes. ❂ *Map L3 • Open Apr–Sep: 10am–noon & 2–4pm Mon–Fri, 10am–noon Sat • Free*

5 Guido Gezelle-museum
Rustic home of one of the best-loved poets in Dutch (and Flemish), the priest Guido Gezelle (1830–99). ❂ *Rolweg 64 • Map M2 • Open 9:30am–12:30pm & 1:30–5pm Tue–Sun • Adm charge*

6 Schuttersgilde Sint-Sebastiaan
This historic archers' guildhouse still functions as an archery club. ❂ *Carmersstraat 174 • Map M2 • 050 33 16 26 • Open Apr–Sep: 10am–noon Tue–Thu, noon–5pm Sat; Oct–Mar: 2pm–5pm Tue–Thu & Sun • Admission charge*

7 Jeruzalemkerk and the Kantcentrum
A real curiosity – a 15th-century private chapel inspired by pilgrimages to Jerusalem. Next door is the Kantcentrum (Lace Centre). ❂ *Peperstraat 3a • Map L3 • Open 10am–noon & 2–6pm Mon–Fri, 10am–noon & 2–5pm Sat. Closed Sun & public hols • Admission charge*

8 Windmills on the Kruisvest
Two of the city's four remaining windmills – Sint-Janshuismolen and Koeleweimolen – are open to the public. ❂ *Map M2 • Open May–Sep: 9:30am–12:30pm & 1:30–5pm Tue–Sun • Admission charge*

9 Kruispoort
One of only four surviving gates of the city walls. ❂ *Map M3*

10 Muur der Doodge-schotenen
A bullet-marked wall commemorates a dozen men executed by the German army during World War I. ❂ *Map M3*

Left **Chocoladehuisje** Right **Saturday morning market, 't Zand**

Shopping

1 Steenstraat and Zuidzandstraat
The main shopping area links the Markt to 't Zand. Clothes, shoes, chocolates – they're all here. ⊗ *Map K4*

2 Zilverpand
This warren of arcades between Zuidzandstraat and Noordzandstraat consists mainly of clothes boutiques. ⊗ *Map K4*

3 Chocoladehuisje
There are chocolate shops at every turn in Bruges. The big names are on Steenstraat and Zuidzandstraat, but try the Chocoladehuisje for its imaginative (sometimes lewd) designs. ⊗ *Wollestraat 15 • Map K4*

4 The Bottle Shop
Bruges has two well-known breweries, De Gouden Boom and De Halve Maan. The Bottle Shop sells their beers, plus the full Belgian range. ⊗ *Wollestraat 13 • Map K4*

5 The Little Lace Shop
There are still some lacemakers in Bruges, though not the 10,000 there were in 1840. For the genuine article go to a reliable outlet such as this, the oldest (founded 1923) and smallest. ⊗ *Markt 11 • Map K4*

6 The Tintin Shop
Good for the whole gamut of Tintin merchandise. ⊗ *Steenstraat 3 • Map K4*

7 Huis Van Loocke
Bruges is so picturesque that it attracts numerous artists, and several excellent shops cater for their needs. This one has been run by the same family for three generations. ⊗ *Ezelstraat 17 • Map L4*

8 Pollentier-Maréchal
This fine shop sells old prints, many of them of Bruges. ⊗ *Sint-Salvatorskerkhof 8 • Map K5*

9 Markets
General markets are in the Markt (Wednesday mornings) and on 't Zand (Saturday mornings). There is also a small but magical Christmas market in the Markt. Flea markets are held weekend afternoons on Dijver and at the Vismarkt. ⊗ *Map J4, K4, L4*

10 Supermarkets
The major supermarkets (such as Louis Delhaize) are in the suburbs, but a few small ones, such as Profi, lie within the city. ⊗ *Oude Burg 22 • Map K4*

ft **De Proeverie** Right **Café Vlissinghe**

Cafés, Tearooms and Bars

De Garre
A famous old *staminee* (pub), at the foot of a folksy little alleyway. Also serves light snacks. *De Garre 1 (off Breidelstraat) • Map K4*

Café Vlissinghe
Said to be the oldest Bruges tavern, founded 1515. Van Dyck apparently met local painters here. Serves light lunches. There's a boules court in the garden. ⊗ *Blekerstraat 2 • Map L3 • Closed Mon & Tue*

De Proeverie
This delightful little coffee shop belongs to the chocolatier opposite: hot chocolate is a speciality. ⊗ *Katelijnestraat 6 • Map K5*

La Plaza
A glamorous café-bar, frequented by an equally glamorous clientele. Drinks, cocktails and delicious light meals. ⊗ *Kuipersstraat 13 • Map K3*

Wijnbar Est
A tiny, red brick house that backs onto the canal with live jazz every Sunday. Serves snacks and an excellent selection of wines. ⊗ *Braambergstraat 7 • Map L4 • 050 33 38 39 • Closed Tue, Wed*

Café "De Versteende Nacht"
Bruges has limited night life, but this jazz café has a welcoming crowd and good basic cooking. ⊗ *Langestraat 11 • Map L3 • 050 34 32 93*

Joey's Café
A fun café-bar with low-lit tables and comfy chairs. Hosts occasional free concerts. ⊗ *Zilverpand (off Zuidzandstraat) • Map K4*

't Brugs Beertje
One of the great beer pubs, serving no fewer than 300 types of beer. If you can't make your mind up, just ask the bar staff. If you want to learn more, try one of their beer seminars. ⊗ *Kemelstraat 5 • Map K4 • Closed Wed*

Lokkedize
A laid-back pub serving good beer, and wholesome snacks and meals. Live jazz and other music are regularly staged. ⊗ *Korte Vuldersstraat 33 • Map K5 • 050 33 44 50 • Closed Mon & Tue*

In de Plantenmarkt
Just off the Markt, this is one of the few genuine bars – as opposed to brasseries – in central Bruges and so popular with the locals. ⊗ *Sint-Amandsstraat 2 • Map K4*

Left **Saint Amour** Right **Den Dyver**

Restaurants

De Karmeliet
With three Michelin stars, this is among Belgium's top restaurants. Exquisite. ® *Langestraat 19 • Map L3 • 050 33 82 59 • Closed Sun & Mon • €€€€€*

Patrick Devos "De Zilveren Pauw"
A restaurant cherished for chef Patrick Devos' creative touch, in an elegant *belle époque* house. ® *Zilverstraat 41 • Map K4 • 050 33 55 66 • Closed Sat L, Sun • €€€€€*

Saint Amour
Dine in candle-lit brick-lined vaults. Chef Johan Nelissen has twice been voted best chef in Flanders. ® *Oude Burg 14 • Map K4 • 050 33 71 72 • Closed Mon, Tue • €€€€*

Den Gouden Karpel
A fine fish restaurant beside the Vismarkt (fish market), with an excellent fish-shop/*traiteur* next door. ® *Huidenvettersplein 4 • Map L4 • 050 33 34 94 • Closed Mon • €€€*

Florentijn
Ambitious French cuisine, contemporary art, stylish design and over 300 wines combine for a memorable meal. ® *Academiestraat 1 • Map K3 • 050 67 75 33 • Closed Sun, Mon • €€€€€*

Rock Fort
Pared-down modern interior in an old family house. The young team brings flair to contemporary cuisine. ® *Langestraat 15 • Map L3 • 050 33 41 13 • Closed Sat & Sun • €€€€*

Den Dyver
A paradise for beer pilgrims: most of the dishes are cooked with Belgian beer, and come with a selected beer, demonstrating an astounding range of flavours. ® *Dijver 5 • Map L4 • 050 33 60 69 • Closed Wed, Thu L • €€€€*

Den Amand
A small restaurant serving inventive dishes of worldwide inspiration. ® *Sint-Amandsstraat 4 • Map K4 • 050 34 01 22 • Closed Sun & Wed D • €€*

't Begijntje
This popular restaurant/tearoom is one of Bruges' most delightful. Try the splendid fish soup. ® *Walstraat 11 • Map K5 • 050 33 00 89 • Closed Tue, Wed • €€*

Resto Mojo
An informal brasserie with friendly waiters and an interesting menu, including ostrich carpaccio and octopus tagliatelli. ® *Schaarstraat 4 • Map M4 • 050 68 05 09 • Closed Tue, Wed • €€€*

Bruges is an excellent place to try out classic Belgian dishes
See p57

Price Categories

For a three course meal for one with half a bottle of wine (or equivalent meal), taxes and extra charges.

€ under €30
€€ €30–€40
€€€ €40–€50
€€€€ €50–€60
€€€€€ over €60

Nieuw Museum

10 Lunch Stops, Brasseries, Bistros

Bistro de Pompe
This very popular bistro serves an excellent value weekday lunch menu. On offer are hearty meals, salads, snacks and crêpes. *Kleine Sint-Amandstraat 2 • Map K4 • 050 61 66 18 • Closed Mon • €€*

Het Dagelijks Brood
Or "Le Pain Quotidien" in French. Part of an esteemed chain providing wholesome sandwiches in crusty bread, plus pâtisserie and other snacks. *Philipstockstraat 1 • Map K4 • Closed Tue • €*

Taverne De Verloren Hoek
A traditional, pleasant and welcoming tavern named after its location in the "Lost Corner" of eastern Bruges. *Carmerstraat 178 • Map M2 • Closed Tue, Wed • €*

De Belegde Boterham
The name translates as "open sandwich", which is exactly what they do – along with soups, salads and cakes. *Kleine Sint-Amandstraat 5 • Map K4 • Open noon–4pm • €*

Salade Folle
A deservedly popular lunch spot and tearoom serving light dishes, home-made cakes, pancakes and waffles. *Walplein 13–14 • Map K5 • 050 34 94 43 • Open 11am–6pm Mon–Tue, 11am–10pm Thu–Sun • €*

Sapristi
This informal café is justifiably proud of its fruit and vegetable juices. A good all-purpose place to call in for one of their speciality sandwiches, a beer or a coffee. *Dweersstraat 4 • Map K4 • Closed Sun • €*

Juliette's
A mother and daughter coffee house serving light lunches; particularly popular with Bruges' female shoppers. *Dweersstraat 15 • Map K4 • Closed Sun • €*

't Nieuw Museum
In this old family-run tavern, the meat is cooked on an open fire (evenings) in a 17th-century fireplace. A delightfully elemental experience. *Hooistraat 42 • Map M4 • 050 33 12 80 • Closed Tue, Wed • €€*

Gran Kaffee de Passage
A wonderfully dingy, candle-lit interior provides an enchanting setting for good beer and solid, good-value Belgian dishes. *Dweersstraat 26 • Map K4 • 050 34 02 32 • €*

Het Andere Idee
A comfortable, well-priced "pasta-bistro", popular with the local crowd. *Hauwerstraat 9 • Map J5 • 050 34 17 89 • Closed Mon, Tue • €*

Left *Adoration of the Mystic Lamb* (central panel) by Hubrecht and Jan van Eyck Right Grasle

Ghent

GHENT HAS MUCH IN COMMON WITH BRUGES. *It is a city with a rich legacy of medieval buildings and art treasures inherited from its days a a semi-autonomous and prosperous trading centre. The tranquil waters of its canals mirror the step-gables of its old guildhouses and the tall spires of its centuries-old skyline. Unlike Bruges, however, historically prosperous Ghent took on a new lease of life as Belgium's first industrial city in the early 19th century. It is also home to a large and famous university. These factors have endowed the city with a scale, bustle, and youthful verve that have shaped its character. Ghent has an elegant grandeur, symbolized by its cathedral, theatres and opera house; but it also has an intimacy, and the web of its medieval street plan – including Europe's largest pedestrianized zone – makes this a perfect city for wandering. It is no surprise, perhaps, that Ghent is the preferred city of many regular visitors to Flanders.*

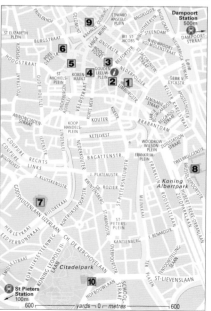

Sint-Niklaaskerk

Sights

1. Sint-Baafskathedraal
2. Belfort
3. Stadhuis
4. Sint-Niklaaskerk
5. Graslei and Korenlei
6. Design Museum Gent
7. Bijlokemuseum
8. Klein Begijnhof
9. Het Huis van Alijn
10. Museum voor Schone Kunsten and SMAK

For Ghent tourist information visit www.gent.be

Sint-Baafskathedraal

St Bavo, or Bavon, was a
[loc]al 7th-century saint. The
[cat]hedral named after him dates
[ba]ck to the 10th century, but
[mo]st of it is Gothic, built over
[thr]ee centuries after 1290.
[Ou]tstanding are the grandiose
[Ba]roque-Rococo pulpit of oak
[an]d marble (1741–5) and the
[ch]urch's greatest treasure the
[mu]lti-panelled, 15th-century
[alt]arpiece, *The Adoration of the
[M]ystic Lamb* by Hubrecht and
[Ja]n van Eyck *(see pp26–7)*. ◈
[Sin]t-Baafsplein • Map Q2 • 09 269 20 45
[• O]pen Apr–Oct: 8:30am–6pm Mon–Sat,
[1]0am–6pm Sun; Nov–Mar: 8:30am–
[5p]m Mon–Sat, 9:30am–5pm Sun (only
[op]en to non-worshippers after 1pm Sun)
[• A]dmission charge (Mystic Lamb only)

Belfort

Ghent's belfry is a prominent
[lan]dmark, rising 91 m (299 ft) to
[th]e gilded dragon on the tip of
[its] spire. It was built in 1380–81
[an]d served for centuries as look-
[ou]t tower, clock and alarm. It
[ho]uses a 54-bell carillon, which
[is] used for regular concerts. There
[is] a lift to the top. ◈ Emile Braun-
[ple]in • Map Q2 • Open 15 Apr–15 Nov:
[10]am–1pm, 2–6pm daily • Adm charge

[Thr]one room, Stadhuis

Sint-Baafskathedraal

Stadhuis

The impressive town hall
was the scene of some of the
great landmarks in the city's
history. Inside is a series of
council chambers, still in use
today – some dating back to the
15th century, others refurbished
during restoration after 1870. ◈
Botermarkt 1 • Map Q2 • Open Jun–Oct:
2pm Mon–Thu (guided tours only, from
Belfort tourist office) • Admission charge

Sint-Niklaaskerk

St Nicholas, Bishop of Myra,
was patron saint of merchants,
and this was the merchants'
church. Built in the 13th to 15th
centuries, it is Belgium's best
example of the austere style
called Scheldt Gothic. ◈
Cataloniëstraat • Map Q2 • Open
10am–5pm Tue–Sun, 2–5pm Mon • Free

Graslei and Korenlei

The Graslei and Korenlei are
departure points for canal trips.
The two quays are lined with the
step-gabled guildhouses of
merchants and tradesmen that
date back to the 12th century.
Sint Michielsbrug, the bridge at
the southern end, offers the best
views of the city. ◈ Map P2

6 Design Museum Gent
This museum is a must for anyone with the slightest interest in furniture, furnishings and interior decoration. Housed in a grand 18th-century mansion, plus an uncompromisingly modern extension, it provides a tour through changing European styles from the 17th century to the present. The Art Nouveau collection is particularly rewarding, with work by Horta, Gallé and Lalique. ◈ *Jan Breydelstraat 5 • Map P1 • 09 267 99 99 • http://design.museum.gent.be • Open 10am–6pm Tue–Sun • Admission charge*

Design Museum

7 Bijlokemuseum
The Abdij van de Bijloke, an old rambling Cistercian convent and hospital, provides the quirky setting for a miscellaneous collection of historical artifacts. Among the cloisters and dormitories you'll find Chinese ceramics, medieval tombs, kitchenware, freemasons' regalia, models of warships, a Louis XIV drawing room, and historical costumes. The convent dates from medieval times, but most of the buildings are 17th-century. ◈ *Godshuizenlaan 2 • Map P4 • 09 225 11 06 • Closed for renovation until Dec 2008 • Admission charge*

Ghent and Charles V
Charles V (1500–58), Holy Roman Emperor, King of Spain, master of much of Europe and the New World, was born in Ghent, and his baptism in Sint-Baafskathedraal was celebrated with a huge feast. But the city's love affair with its famous son went sour when it found itself endlessly squeezed for taxes. A revolt in 1540, and the execution by hanging of its ringleaders, gave rise to the people of Ghent being called the *stroppendragers* ("noose bearers" – a proud symbol of their defiant and independent spirit.

8 Klein Begijnhof
There are three *béguinages (see p86)* in Ghent, but this is by far the prettiest. With step-gabled, whitewashed houses set around a little park and Baroque church, it is a classic of its kind, a fact recognized by its status as a UNESCO World Heritage Site. It was founded as a community of single women in about 1235, and has been continuously occupied, although the residents are no longer *béguines*. Most of the present houses date from the 17th century. ◈ *Lange Violettestraat 208 • Map R4 • Open daily 6am–10pm (or dusk) • Free*

9 Het Huis van Alijn
Just north of the centre of Ghent is a quaint and folksy quarter called the Patershol, a warren of little medieval streets and alleys. This is the backdrop for one of the best folk museums in Belgium (it was formerly called the Museum voor Volkskunde). A huge and fascinating collection of artifacts – toys, games, shoes and crockery, as well as complete shops and craftsmen's workshops – are laid out within almshouses

et around a grassy courtyard.
ıese almshouses were founded
ı 1363 as a children's hospital –
ıt as an act of pure philanthropy
ıt as penance for the murder of
ʋo members of the Alijn family.
 *Kraanlei 65 • Map Q1 • 09 269 23 50
 Open 11am–5pm Tue–Sun • Admission
 ₋arge*

Museum voor Schone Kunsten and SMAK

ıent's two leading museums of
t are a short tram or bus ride
₋uth of the city centre. The
ıseum voor Schone Kunsten
ine Arts Museum) covers
ıinting and sculpture from the
ıiddle Ages up to the early 20th
₋ntury and has a world-class and
₋lectic collection of works by a
ımber of important artists, such
 Hieronymus Bosch, Rogier van
₋r Weyden and Hugo van der
₋es. Opposite the MSK, and
 more ways than one, is the
₋edelijk Museum voor Aktuele
ınst (SMAK), which is Ghent's
ıperb modern art gallery. Its
₋allenging permanent collection
ıd regularly changing temporary
₋hibitions have placed SMAK at
₋ forefront of modern art
ılleries in Europe. ◈ *Citadelpark
 Map Q6 • MSK: 09 240 07 00.*
 ʋw.mskgent.be; SMAK: 09 222 17 03.
 *ʋw.smak.be • Open 10am–6pm
 ₋–Sun • Admission charges*

ıseum voor Schone Kunsten

A Day in Ghent

Morning

🕐 **SMAK** and the **Museum voor Schone Kunsten** *(see left)* make a good double act – a stimulating mixture of fine art and pure provocation, from world-class artists. Get these under your belt early in the day (note that they're closed on Mon). Trams 1 and 10 run from the central Korenmarkt to Charles de Kerchovelaan, from where you can walk through or beside the **Citadelpark** to the museums. These will absorb the greater part of the morning; you can break for refreshments at SMAK's café. For lunch, head back into the city centre. The Korenmarkt is equidistant from two enticing and contrasting lunch options: **The House of Eliott** *(see p99)*, and the medieval **Groot Vleeshuis** *(see p98)*.

Afternoon

Now go to **Sint-Baafskathedraal** to see the **Mystic Lamb** *(see pp26–7)*. Then you can go up the **Belfort** *(see p95)* to get a view over the city. Now it's back to the Korenmarkt, stopping off at the **Sint-Niklaaskerk** *(see p95)*, then over to the **Graslei** and **Korenlei** *(see p95)* to drink in the views. This could be the time to take a canal trip. From the Korenlei, walk along Jan Breydelstraat and take the first right into Rekeligestraat to reach the **Gravensteen** (Castle of the Counts). Then cross the Zuivelbrug and take Meerseniersstraat to the **Vrijdagmarkt** (Friday Market) for beer at **Dulle Griet** *(see p98)* and chips with mayonnaise at **Frituur Jozef** *(see p99)*.

Left **'t Dreupelkot** Right **Groot Vleeshuis**

Shops, Cafés and Bars

1 Mageleinstraat and Koestraat
Ghent claims to have the largest pedestrianized zone of any city in Europe, making shopping all the more agreeable. Most chain stores are in Veldstraat and Lange Munt, but there's more charm around the quieter Mageleinstraat and Koestraat. ✪ Map Q2

2 Post Plaza
The palatial Neo-Gothic former post office has been cleverly turned into a modern mall of high-profile boutiques. ✪ Korenmarkt 16 • Map Q2

3 t'Vosken
Dramatic black and white café-bar located by the cathedral. Traditional brasserie-style food includes rabbit stew with prunes. ✪ St-Baafsplein 19 • Map Q2

4 Dulle Griet
One of the celebrated "beer academies" of Belgium, with 250 beers on offer. Note the basket in which you must deposit a shoe as security when drinking Kwak, a beer served in a cherished glass. ✪ Vrijdagmarkt 50 • Map Q1

5 Pole Pole
A dynamic cocktail bar (evenings only): one side is Mexican, the other side African. The African phrase

pole pole translates as "take it easy". ✪ Lammerstraat 8 • Map Q3

6 't Dreupelkot
A folksy waterfront bar which serves only *jenever*, a form of gin, variously flavoured with fruit, vanilla, even chocolat ✪ Groentenmarkt 12 • Map Q1

7 Groot Vleeshuis
This centre for East Flemis food – part restaurant, part deli catessen – is sensationally locate in a medieval butchers' hall. ✪ Groentenmarkt 7 • Map Q1 • 09 223 23 • Restaurant closed Mon • €

8 Brooderie
The smell of freshly baked bread wafts around this rustic-style eatery serving sandwiche and light vegetarian fare. ✪ Jan Breydelstraat 8 • Map P1 • Closed Mon

9 Hot Club de Gand
This hidden jewel at the en of a narrow alley, opposite the Butchers' Hall, is tricky to find, but the live music most evenings makes the search worthwhile. ✪ Groentenmarkt 15B • Map Q1 • 0498 54 11

10 Het Brood-Huys
A welcoming café and tearoom, specializing in wholesome bread and pâtisserie. ✪ Jakobijnenstraat 12 • M P2 • Closed Mon • €

e House of Eliott

Price Categories

For a three course meal for one with half a bottle of wine (or equivalent meal), taxes and extra charges.

€ under €30
€€ €30–€40
€€€ €40–€50
€€€€ €50–€60
€€€€€ over €60

10 Restaurants

1 Belga Queen
The historic 13th-century ilding, elegant decor and the ality of the locally-sourced od, create a high-end feel at is contemporary restaurant. ◎ aslei 10 • Map P2 • 09 280 01 00 • €€€€

2 Patyntje
A trek to the suburbs is paid by this beautiful colonial-yle house overlooking the River ie. Exquisite French-Belgian isine with Eastern touches. ◎ rdunakaai 91 • 09 222 32 73 • €€€

3 Brasserie Pakhuis
Run by celebrated restaurant signer Antoine Pinto, Pakhuis big and very popular – so serve! ◎ Schuurkenstraat 4 • Map P2 09 223 55 55 • Closed Sun • €€€

4 Keizershof
The building has been reno-ted in upbeat modern style, t the restaurant within still rves traditional Belgian dishes. Vrijdagmarkt 47 • Map Q1 • 09 223 46 • Closed Sun–Mon • €€

5 Korenlei Twee
This 18th-ntury dock-side wn house, serves eals using ingredi-ts from the local h and meat mar-ts. Good value and cellent wine. ◎ renlei 2 • Map P2 09 224 00 73 • Closed n, Tue • €€€

6 Eat@café
All black and white and chrome, and as modern as its name would suggest. Drinks and well-made light meals with a touch of style. ◎ Vlaanderenstraat 129 • Map R3 • 09 233 36 00 • €€

7 Coeur d'Artichaut
Pared-down elegance in an old mansion, with patio. Light, wholesome, international cuisine prepared to high standards of excellence. ◎ Onderbergen 6 • Map P2 • 09 225 33 18 • Closed Sun, Mon • €€€€

8 Theatercafé De Foyer
This excellent brasserie is dramatically located within the grand 19th-century Koninklijke Nederlandse Schouwburg (theatre), with a balcony over-looking Sint-Baafskathedraal. Crêpes and waffles are served in the afternoons; buffet brunch on Sundays. ◎ Sint-Baafsplein 17 • Map Q2 • 09 225 32 75 • €€

9 The House of Eliott
Joyously eccentric pseudo-Edwardian restaurant overlooking the canal. ◎ Jan Breydelstraat 36 • Map P1 • 09 225 21 28 • Closed Tue, Wed • €€€€

10 Frituur Jozef
Old-established chip stand serving perfect chips (fries) and all the trim-mings. ◎ Vrijdagmarkt • Map Q1

When in Ghent, you should try the city's classic dish, Waterzooi
See p57

Left **Koninklijk Museum voor Schone Kunsten** Right **Rubenshuis**

Antwerp

SET ON THE BROAD RIVER SCHELDT, *at the gateway to the North Sea, Antwerp is one of the leading trading cities of northern Europe; and in the early 17th century it was one of the great cultural centres too. The city, though, has had its share of suffering – battered by the religious wars of the 16th century, cut off from the North Sea by treaty with the Netherlands from 1648 to 1795, and bombed in World War II. These historical ups and downs have endowed the city with a keen edge, like its famous diamonds. This dynamic energy is seen today in its hip bars, restaurants and nightclubs.*

🔟 Sights

1. Grote Markt
2. Onze-Lieve-Vrouwekathedraal
3. Rubenshuis
4. Koninklijk Museum voor Schone Kunsten
5. Nationaal Scheepvaartmuseum
6. Museum Plantin-Moretus
7. Vleeshuis
8. Sint-Jacobskerk
9. Rockoxhuis
10. Museum Mayer van den Bergh

Statue of Brabo, Grote Markt

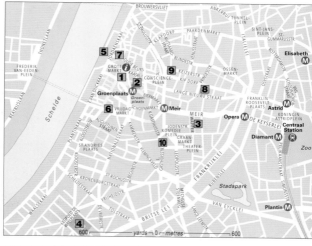

Preceding pages **Selection of Belgian pralines**

ote Markt

Grote Markt

The main square of Antwerp one of the great gilded arenas Belgium. The city authorities ade a virtue of its unusual dog-leg" shape and slope by ommissioning sculptor Jef ambeaux (1852–1908) to create n eye-catching fountain, placed f-centre, with its water spilling ut directly onto the cobbles. It epicts Brabo, a legendary oman soldier who freed the ort of Antwerp by defeating the ant Antigoon and throwing his evered hand (*hand-werpen*) into e river. The Italian-influenced adhuis (town hall) dominates e square. Built in the 1560s, its and horizontals are offset by e upward curve of the roof-orners, like a smile. ◎ *Map T1 • adhuis: guided tours only (ask at tourist fice, Grote Markt 13) • Adm charge*

Onze-Lieve-Vrouwekathedraal

his huge Gothic cathedral ontains several splendid works Rubens (*see pp28–9*).

Rubenshuis

A rare opportunity not only to sit the house and studio of one the great stars of European t, but also to see what a 17th-entury patrician home looked ke (*see pp30–31*).

Koninklijk Museum voor Schone Kunsten

Antwerp's fine arts museum is in a similar league to Brussels' equivalent, housing a full range of paintings from early Flemish "Primitives", such as Jan van Eyck, Rogier van der Weyden and Hans Memling, to the Symbolists James Ensor and Rik Wouters. Not surprisingly, special emphasis is placed on Rubens, Jordaens and Van Dyck. The collection is housed in a grand Neo-Classical pile a tram ride or 20-minute walk from the city centre. ◎ *Leopold De Waelplaats • Map S3 • 03 238 78 09 • Open 10am–5pm, Tue–Sat, 10am–6pm Sun. Closed public hols • Admission charge (free on last Wed of the month)*

Nationaal Scheepvaartmuseum

The National Maritime Museum paints a rich portrait of the city's links to the sea, through models, maps, artifacts and a large collection of boats. ◎ *Steenplein 1 • Map T1 • 03 201 93 40 • Museum open 10am–5pm Tue–Sun. Closed public hols • Maritime Park open Easter–end Oct • Admission charge*

Nationaal Scheepvaartmuseum

Museum Plantin-Moretus

6 Museum Plantin-Moretus

Christopher Plantin (c.1520–89) was a French bookbinder who in 1546 came to Antwerp to set up his own printing workshop. It became one of the most influential publishing houses in Europe during the late Renaissance, producing Bibles, maps, scientific books and much else. The museum consists essentially of the printing workshop and home of Plantin and his heirs. It contains a large collection of rare and precious books, and displays of their illustrations. The processes of hot-metal type setting and letterpress printing are also explained. Plantin gave his name to a typeface still widely used today. ◎ *Vrijdagmarkt 22 • Map T2 • 03 221 14 50 • Open 10am–5pm Tue–Sun. Closed Mon & public hols • Admission charge (free last Wed of month)*

The River Scheldt

Old Antwerp lies on the east bank of the River Scheldt (or Schelde). The river is so broad that the modern suburb on the west bank seems utterly remote (it is linked by tunnels). The Scheldt is deep enough to bring large ships to Antwerp's docks to the north of the city. This easy access to the North Sea has made Antwerp Europe's second largest port.

---

7 Vleeshuis

With its turrets and towers and Gothic detail, the "Meat House" is one of the most beautiful and curious buildings Antwerp. Built in 1501–4 as the guildhouse of the butchers and meat market, it is now used as a museum of music. From street singers to concert hall, the Vleeshuis charts the history of the city through its many forms of musical expression, using historical instruments, including harpsichords made by the famous Ruckers family, manuscripts and a bell foundry. ◎ *Vleeshouwersstraat 38–40 • Map T1 • 03 292 61 00 • Open 10am–5pm Tue–Sun • Admission charge (free last Wed of month)*

Vleeshuis

8 Sint-Jacobskerk

Of all the churches in Antwerp, the church of St James is noted for having the richest interior – and for being the burial place of Rubens. It was built in late Gothic style in the 15th and 16th centuries by architects who also worked on the cathedral. The church contains work by leading sculptors of the 17th century, such as Lucas Faydherbe, Artus Quellinus and Hendrik Verbruggen, as well as paintings by Rubens, Jordaens and Van Dyck. ◈ *Lange Nieuwstraat 3–75 • Map U2 • 02 232 10 32 • Open 1 Apr–31 Oct: 2–5pm Mon–Sun • Closed 1e • Admission charge*

Rockoxhuis

Come here for a glimpse of the grace and elegance of 17th-century patrician style. A series of rooms contains a fine collection of furniture, paintings and artifacts. The house is named after its owner, city mayor Nicholas Rockox (1560–1640), a philanthropist and friend and patron of Rubens. There are paintings and drawings by Rubens, Jordaens and Van Dyck, as well as work by Frans Snyders (1579–1657), who lived next door. ◈ *Keizerstraat 12 • Map U1 • 03 201 92 50 • Open 10am–5pm Tue–Sun • Admission charge (free on last Wed of every month)*

10 Museum Mayer van den Bergh

Fritz Mayer van den Bergh (1858–91) was an avid collector of art and curios. When he died, his mother created a museum to display his collections – some 5,000 items in all. They include tapestries, furniture, ivories, stained glass, paintings and coins. ◈ *Lange Gasthuisstraat 19 • Map T2 • 03 232 42 37 • Open 10am–5pm Tue–Sun • Adm charge (free on last Wed of the month)*

Museum Mayer van den Bergh

A Day in Antwerp

Morning

🕐 This day of gentle ambling takes in many of the key sights of Antwerp, as well as some of the best shopping streets. Start off at the **Vleeshuis** and head for the old city centre – the **Grote Markt** *(see p103)* – and the **cathedral** *(see pp28–9)*. Now thread your way to Wijngaard-straat, and the fetching ensemble of the **Sint-Carolus Borromeuskerk** *(see p106)*, before heading on to the **Rockoxhuis** *(see left)* in Keizerstraat. After this, walk south along Katelijnevest to the **Meir**. The tower block to your right, with KBC on its crest, is the **Boerentoren**, the highest building in Europe when constructed in 1932. Head down the Meir to the **Rubenshuis** *(see pp30–31)*; you can lunch here, or if you prefer at the **Grand Café Horta** *(see p108)*.

Afternoon

Now you've done the culture, you can wander the neighbourhood's shopping streets *(see p107)*. **Schuttershofstraat** is a good place to start. It leads to Huidevettersstraat, the Nieuwe Gaanderij Arcade, Korte Gasthuis-straat and Lombardenvest. If you are up for more museums, the excellent **Museum Mayer van den Bergh** *(see left)* and the **Maagdenhuis** *(see p106)* are just to the south. Alternatively, head for Nationalestraat and Dries van Noten's outlet, the beautiful **Modepaleis**, *(see p107)*, and then down to **Pier 19** *(see p108)* or **De Vagant** *(see p109)* for some refreshments.

Left **Sint-Carolus Borromeuskerk** Right **Diamond polishing at the Diamantmuseum**

Best of the Rest

1 MAS (Museum Aan de Stroom)

A bold, waterfront museum focusing on Antwerp's global connections as a major trading port. MAS also includes the superb collection of the former Ethnographic Museum. ◎ *Hanzestedenplaats1* • *Map U1* • *03 206 09 40* • *www.mas.be* • *Open 10am–5pm Tue–Sun. Closed public hols* • *Adm charge*

2 Diamantmuseum

Tracing the diamond from mine to tiara. ◎ *Koningin Astridplein 19–23* • *Map V2* • *03 202 48 90* • *www.diamantmuseum.be* • *Open 10am–5:30pm Thu–Tue. Closed Jan* • *Adm charge*

3 Museum voor Fotografie

Antwerp's excellent museum of photography and historical artifacts also contains the MUHKA *(see below)* film museum, showing classic films from around the world. ◎ *Waalsekaai 47* • *Map S3* • *03 242 93 00* • *www.fotomuseum.be*

4 MUHKA

A former warehouse contains the dynamic, cutting-edge Museum voor Hedendaagse Kunst (contemporary art). ◎ *Leuvenstraat 32* • *Map S3* • *03 238 59 60* • *www.muhka.be* • *Open 10am–5pm Tue–Sun. Closed public hols* • *Adm charge*

5 Sint-Pauluskerk

Gothic and Baroque fight it out in this endearing church. ◎ *Veemarkt 14* • *Map T1* • *03 231 33 21* • *Open Easter & May–Sep: 2–5pm daily*

6 Sint-Carolus Borromeuskerk

Celebrated for its Baroque façade and its tragic loss of 39 Rubens paintings. ◎ *Hendrik Conscienceplein* • *Map T1* • *03 231 37 51* • *Open 10am–5pm Mon–Sat, 2–6pm Sun*

7 Centraal Station

Architect Louis Delacenserie created this grand Neo-Classical station in 1905. ◎ *Map V2*

8 Cogels-Osylei

In the late 19th century, the area around Cogels-Osylei became a showcase for opulent architecture – extraordinary.

9 Maagdenhuis

Quirky museum in an old orphanage. ◎ *Lange Gasthuisstraat 33* • *Map T3* • *03 223 56 20* • *Open 10am–5pm Mon, Wed–Fri, 1–5pm Sat–Sun. Closed public hols* • *Adm charge*

10 ModeMuseum (MoMu)

A museum of *haute couture.* ◎ *Nationalestraat 28* • *Map T2* • *03 470 27 70* • *www.momu.be* • *Open 10am–6pm Tue–Sun, 10am–9pm Thu* • *Adm charge*

Left **Het Modepaleis** Right **Walter**

10 Shopping

1 Meir
The main shopping street is a broad pedestrianized avenue, fronted largely by high-street chain stores. ◎ *Map U2*

2 Pelikaanstraat
Wall-to-wall diamond and jewellery shops in the Jewish quarter. Fascinating, partly because there's nothing romantic about it – the gems are commodities like any other. ◎ *Map V2*

3 Nieuwe Gaanderij Arcade
A good place to snoop for fashion at a slightly lower pitch than the designer boutiques. ◎ *Between Huidevettersstraat and Korte Gasthuisstraat • Map T2*

4 Shopping Center Grand Bazar
An elegant modern arcade shares space with the Hilton Hotel in the shell of a former department store. ◎ *Groenplaats • Map T2*

5 Korte Gasthuisstraat and Lombardenvest
The heart of a pedestrianized area which contains attractive specialist shops of all kinds. ◎ *Map T2*

6 Schuttershofstraat
Another street of recherché boutiques and shoe shops, including a branch of the ultimate Belgian accessories manufacturer Delvaux. Smell that leather! ◎ *Map U3*

7 Het Modepaleis
This elegant *belle époque* "flat iron" building is the main outlet for one of Antwerp's most fêted fashion designers, Dries van Noten. ◎ *Nationalestraat 16 • Map T2*

8 Walter
What looks more like an art gallery than a clothes shop is the showcase for fashion designer Walter van Bierendonck, as well as other select labels. ◎ *Sint-Antoniusstraat 12 • Map T2*

9 Ann Demeulemeester
A stone's throw from the MUHKA modern art gallery, Demeulemeester's shop displays the uncompromising edge that has placed her at the forefront of fashion. ◎ *Leopold de Waelplaats/Verlatstraat • Map S3*

10 Louis
Famous boutique carrying the top names. ◎ *Lombardenstraat 2 • Map T2*

Price Categories

For a three course meal for one with half a bottle of wine (or equivalent meal), taxes and extra charges.	**€** under €30
	€€ €30–€40
	€€€ €40–€50
	€€€€ €50–€60
	€€€€€ over €60

P. Preud'Homme

Cafés and Restaurants

Gin-Fish
On the site of former fish restaurant De Matelote, Gin-Fish offers a no-options three-course set menu. ◊ Haarstraat 9 • Map T2 • 03 231 32 07 • Closed lunch • €€€€€

P. Preud'Homme
Amid gilded grandeur, pampered guests feast on lobster, game and other seasonal delights. ◊ Suikerrui 28 • Map T1 • 03 233 42 00 • €€€€

Le Docks Café
Inventive, multi-layered interior by celebrated designer Antoine Pinto. Choose from oyster snacks or full Franco–Italian dishes. ◊ Jordaenskaai 7 • Map T1 • 03 226 63 30 • €€€

Zuiderterras
A landmark building over the River Scheldt, containing an elegant, first-class brasserie. ◊ Ernest van Dijckkaai 37 • Map T2 • 03 234 12 75 • €€€

Pier 19
This warehouse conversion in the old dockland area north of the city houses a lounge club (DJs Thu–Sat), restaurant and lunch spot. ◊ Brouwersvliet 19 • Map T1 • 03 288 78 61 • Closed Sun • €€€

Het Vermoeide Model
This brasserie-restaurant creates an intimate mood with medieval beams and live piano music. ◊ Lijnwaadmarkt 2 • Map T2 • 03 233 52 61 • Closed Mon • €€

Rooden Hoed
Apparently the oldest restaurant in Antwerp, so central you can hear the cathedral orga from the terrace. ◊ Oude Koornma 25 • Map T2 • 03 233 28 44 • €€€

Grand Café Horta
A dynamic space created using metal salvaged from Victor Horta's celebrated Art Nouveau Volkshuis in Brussels, demolished in 1965. ◊ Hopland 2 • Map U2 • 03 232 28 15 • €€€

Dôme Sur Mer
Floor-to-ceiling windows an a marble bar make an impressi setting for this hugely popular fish restaurant in the Zurenborg ◊ Arendstraat 1 • Map V3 • 03 281 743 • Closed Sun, Mon • €€€€

Brasserie Appelmans
Brasserie-style dining in a 12th-century building with class Belgian dishes made from local sourced ingredients. ◊ Papenstraa 1 • Map T2 • 03 226 20 22 • €€€

Recommend your favourite restaurant on traveldk.com

Left **Het Elfde Gebod** Right **Den Engel**

🔟 Bars and Clubs

Café d'Anvers
House, soul, disco and funk in an old red-light district warehouse. The best-known – and, to many, the best – disco in town. ⊗ Verversrui 15 • Map T1 • 03 226 3870

Stereo Sushi
Trendy club with a mix of international DJs and home-grown talent. ⊗ Luikstraat 6 • Map S3

Cafe Local
A glamorous complex of themed Latin-American-style areas: Cuban market, high street, ballroom. It holds Saturday-night salsa, and Latin-American "fiestas" on advertised dates. ⊗ Waalsekaai 5 • Map S3 • 003 238 50 04

Red and Blue/ Fill Collins Club
Red and Blue is a men-only club on Saturdays; Fill Collins is a conventional club on Fridays. ⊗ Lange Schipperskapelstraat • Map T1 • Red and Blue 03 213 05 55

Het Elfde Gebod
The name means "The Eleventh Commandment", and the bar's walls are packed with gaudy religious icons. A stairway to heaven? ⊗ Torfbrug 10 • Map T1

Hopper
This jazz bar is very popular with Antwerp's creative-set. The drink to ask for is demi-demi (half cava; half white wine). ⊗ Leopold De Waelstraat 2 • Map S3 • 03 248 49 33

Sips
A chic cocktail bar in the arty dockland area south of the city centre. Cigars are a speciality. ⊗ Gillisplaats 8

Den Engel
A classic Belgian bruine kroeg (brown pub – brown with the patina of age) overlooking the Grote Markt. Try a bolleke (chalice-like glass) of De Koninck, Antwerp's cherished own brew. ⊗ Grote Markt 3 • Map T1

De Muze
A friendly pub with live jazz most evenings until 2 or 3am. Exposed beams and brickwork create a cosy ambience. ⊗ Melkmarkt 15 • Map T2 • 03 226 01 26

De Vagant
A welcoming traditional café-bar offering some 200 types of jenever (gin). The restaurant upstairs specializes in jenever-based dishes. ⊗ Reyndersstraat 25 • Map T2 • 03 233 15 38

STREETSMART

Left **Accessing information at an internet café** Right **Tourist information sign**

TOP 10 General Information

1 Choose Your City
Brussels, Bruges, Ghent or Antwerp? All share historical interest, art galleries, good hotels and restaurants, and enjoyable shopping. But each is different. Brussels: vibrant capital. Bruges: medieval wonder. Ghent: venerable university town. Antwerp: city of trade. Look at the introductions to each city above *(pp66–9, 76–9, 84–7, 94–7 and 102–5)*, and see which one most strikes a chord.

2 Languages
The people of Bruges, Ghent and Antwerp speak Dutch; in Brussels they speak French or Dutch (some speak the old dialect hybrid Bruxellois). Generally English is fairly widely understood. There is a third official Belgian language, German, spoken in the eastern cantons.

3 National Tourist Offices
There are Belgian tourist offices in most western capitals, operated by the two main tourist authorities: Tourism Flanders–Brussels; and the Belgian Tourist Office–Brussels-Ardennes.
In London: Tourism Flanders–Brussels, Flanders House, 1a Cavendish Square, London W1G 0LD. Information line: 0207 307 7738. Brochure ordering line: 0800 954 5245.
www.visitflanders.co.uk

In New York: Belgian Tourist Office, 220 East 42nd Street, Suite 3402, New York NY 10017. 212 758 8130. www.visitbelgium.com

4 City Tourist Offices
Each city has its own tourist office *(see panel)*, providing detailed local information and assisting with hotel reservations.

5 Internet
National and city tourist offices have useful websites *(see panel)*, providing details of key attractions, events, restaurants and hotels, as well as maps and other links.

6 Weather
Belgian weather is typical for northern Europe: a mix of sunshine and rain, distributed across the four seasons. Average seasonal temperatures range from 1°C (34°F) in winter to 19°C (66°F) in summer.

7 What to Pack
Regarding clothing, assume the worst in weather and you'll be fine. Pack comfortable shoes – you will be walking.

8 Time Difference
Belgium is on Central European Time, one hour ahead of GMT. It observes Daylight Saving Time, so remains one hour ahead of the UK, and six hours ahead of New York, all year round.

9 Electricity and Outlets
Belgium runs on 220 volt AC, using two-pin plugs. The current is fine for most British equipment, but American visitors will need a transformer.

10 Public Holidays
Belgian public holidays are: New Year's Day; Easter Monday; Labour Day (1 May); Ascension Day (6th Thu after Easter); Whit Monday (7th Mon after Easter); Festival of the Flemish Community (11 July, Flanders only); National (Independence) Day (21 July); Assumption (15 Aug); All Saints' Day (1 Nov); Armistice Day (11 Nov); Christmas Day. Banks and post offices will remain closed; shops and museums may stay open.

City Tourist Offices

Brussels
Hôtel de Ville, Grand Place • Map C3
• 02 513 89 40
• www.brussels international.be

Bruges
Concertgebouw, 'T Zand 34 • Map J5
• 050 44 46 46
• www.brugge.be

Ghent
Belfort, St-Baafsplein
• Map Q2 • 09 266 56 60 • www.visitghent.be

Antwerp
Grote Markt 13 • Map T1 • 03 232 01 03
• www.antwerpen.be

Sign up for DK's email newsletter on traveldk.com

Left Checking in Right **Trains at the Gare du Midi, Brussels**

10 Getting There

1 Visas and Entry Requirements

You need a passport to enter Belgium, valid at least three months beyond the end of your stay. Citizens of the EU, the USA, Australia and New Zealand need no visa if staying for less than 90 days. Citizens of other countries should consult their Belgian embassy for information.

2 Customs and Allowances

Most goods can be transported between EU countries, including wines, spirits and tobacco, provided they are for your own personal use, and in quantities that reflect this. For non-EU citizens flying to Belgium, national limits apply.

3 By Air

Most international flights arrive at Zaventem airport, 14 km (9 miles) north-east of Brussels. There are train links from Brussels to Bruges, Ghent and Antwerp. Some airlines go to Charleroi (also called "Brussels South"), 40 km (25 miles) south of the city. There are also small airports at Antwerp and Ostend.

4 Zaventem Airport

You can reach central Brussels from Zaventem airport by taxi or by train. A bus service ("Airport Line") connects the airport to Brussels' European Quarter.

5 By Train

The central hub of Belgium's rail network is Brussels, which has three main stations: the Gare du Midi (Zuidstation), the Gare Centrale (Centraal Station) and the Gare du Nord (Noordstation). Eurostar trains from London (as well as international TGV and Thalys trains) arrive at the Gare du Midi. There are good train connections with Bruges, Ghent and Antwerp (for onward journeys, see p114).

6 Brussels Gare du Midi

The station is connected by bus, tram, metro and taxi to all part of Brussels, but the pictogram signposting is virtually indecipherable; you may need help just to get out of the station! Help is at hand at the tourist office in the Eurostar/Thalys hall. ◎ *Map A5*

7 By Car

To bring a car into Belgium, you must carry a valid EU driving licence, or international driving licence, plus insurance and car registration documents. You must also carry a warning triangle and first-aid kit. You will be driving on the right, so adjust the angle of your headlamps if travelling from Britain so that they don't dazzle oncoming drivers.

8 Free Motorways

All the motorways in Belgium are toll-free and most are well-maintained. Almost all are well lit at night.

9 Crossing the English Channel

Travellers from Britain can cross the Channel by ferry, or via the Channel Tunnel *(see panel below)*.

10 By Bus

Eurolines runs a regular bus service from London to Brussels, to Antwerp, to Ghent, and (in summer) to Bruges. There are also bus services that connect the cities of northern Britain to the Hull-Zeebrugge ferry crossing.

Cross Channel Operators in Britain

P&O Ferries
08716 645 645
• www.poferries.com

Sea France
08705 711711
• www.seafrance.com

Norfolkline
0844 847 5042
• www.norfolkline.com

Eurotunnel
0870 535 3535
• www.eurotunnel.com

Eurostar
08705 353 535
• www.eurostar.com

Eurolines
08717 818 181
• www.eurolines.co.uk

Left **Taxis at a taxi rank** Right **Bicycles can be hired throughout Belgium**

🔟 Getting Around

1 Distances Between Cities

Belgium is a small place – hardly larger than Wales or New Hampshire – and the four cities are all in the north of the country. Brussels is the farthest south. Antwerp lies 45 km (28 miles) due north of Brussels; Ghent lies to the west and about 50 km (31 miles) from both Brussels and Antwerp; Bruges lies a further 40 km (25 miles) north-west of Ghent.

2 By Train

Belgium's excellent national rail service, called SNCB in French and NMBS in Dutch, is clean, efficient and reasonably priced. Regular services link all four cities. The website has timetables and ticket prices. 🌐 www.b-rail.be

3 By Car

Belgian drivers used to have a bad reputation – practical driving tests began only in the 1960s. Today they are no worse than any other European drivers; faults such as driving too close on the motorway *(see p121)* are virtually universal. In the cities, take care of trams, which compete fiercely for road space. See also the note on *priorité de droite* on p121.

4 Parking

There is plenty of parking in and around all the cities. The best plan is to use one of the main public car parks, which are well signposted and not too expensive. City centres get clogged with traffic at busy times, and car parking there is limited. Especially in Bruges and Ghent, visitors are encouraged to use outlying car parks.

5 Car Rental

All the main car hire agencies operate in Belgium. Usually you get better value if you book a hire car in your home country, linking it with your flight. Note that all the cities are compact; you don't really need a car unless you want to go touring outside the city limits or travel from one city to another.

6 Taxis

Taxis are available at taxi ranks or can be booked by phone. In Brussels, they can be hailed on the street – but not usually in the other three cities. They cost quite a lot more than public transport. A 10 per cent tip is customary.

7 City Transport

The main transport systems are bus and tram; Brussels also has a Metro (underground railway or subway), and Antwerp an underground tram system called the Pre-Metro. Use the buttons on board trams and buses to indicate that you wish to get off at the next stop, and to open the doors. Public transport in Brussels is operated by STIB (or MIVB); in the other cities the operator is De Lijn. www.stib.be; www.delijn.

8 Buying Tickets

Tickets for public transport cover buses, trams and Metro. Single tickets, a card valid for 10 journeys, or a one-day pass can be bought at ticket booths or stations. Single tickets for buses and trams are also available from the driver. At the start of a journey you have to validate the ticket in the orange machine on board a bus or tram, or on entering a Metro station; it is then valid for a single journey of up to an hour including any changes you need to make.

9 Cycling

Belgians are keen cyclists, but dedicated cycle paths are not common. You can hire bikes and equipment in all the cities. The city tourist offices *(see p112)* will provide details.

10 On Foot

This is probably the best way of all to get around. In all the cities, most of the things you will want to see are close to the centre, and within easy walking distance of one another. Take a pair of sturdy waterproof shoes.

Left Cobbled streets in historic towns can make access difficult **Right** Disabled access sign

10 Tips for Disabled Travellers

Before You Leave

Historic cities such as Brussels, Bruges, Antwerp and Ghent have developed over centuries with scant attention paid to disabled travellers' needs. Although attitudes are changing, adapting the physical environment to meet their needs will take a long time. The tourist authorities have collated information to help disabled people, but there are still large gaps. It is therefore important to do your research before you leave home.

Organizations

Among bodies in the UK providing advice and practical help to disabled travellers are Tripscope, youreable.com and RADAR (Royal Association for Disability and Rehabilitation). Those in the USA include Mobility International, and SATH (Society for Accessible Travel and Hospitality). ✆ www.youreable.com • RADAR: 020 7250 3222. www.radar.org.uk • Mobility International: (541) 343 1284. www. miusa.org • SATH: (212) 447 7284. www.sath.org

Information

City tourist offices hold information on, for example, wheelchair-accessible toilets and facilities for disabled people in hotel rooms, but this is not published in collated form on their websites, so telephone or e-mail the offices (see p112) to find out what help they can offer. Unfortunately, there is currently no central organization in Belgium dealing with information for disabled travellers.

Holiday Companies

Some UK tour operators specialize in travel for disabled people and their companions. Holiday Care has a Benelux guide. Accessible Travel and Leisure (ATL) offers city breaks in Brussels and Bruges. ✆ HolidayCare: 0845 124 9971. www. holidaycare.org.uk • ATL: 01452 729 739. www. accessibletravel.co.uk

Local Attitudes

The Belgians are very sympathetic to the needs of disabled travellers. If you need their help, they will usually be quick to give it. This compensates to some extent for the lack of ramps, adapted bathrooms, wide doors and other aids.

Steps and Cobbles

Many key sites are in historic areas of cities where access is hard for disabled people. Some have been adapted, but others elude practical conversion. Bruges, especially, will never be able totally to adapt its winding staircases, narrow pavements and cobbled streets.

Museums and Galleries

Most larger museums have adequate facilities for disabled people, including wide entrances, ramps, lifts and adapted toilets. Staff are usually helpful; if in doubt about accessibility, telephone before you visit.

Public Transport

The bus, tram and Metro systems, and train stations are generally poorly adapted to use by disabled travellers – although some newer trams have wheelchair access. Tourist offices can offer advice about alternatives, including special taxi services. Belgian Railways also has advice pages on its website. ✆ www.b-rail.be

Accommodation

Many modern or recently renovated hotels have one or more rooms with special facilities for disabled and wheelchair-bound people. These are indicated in tourist office brochures and on the hotels' websites.

Restaurants

Although restaurants are under pressure to improve their provision, the number of those with full disabled access and facilities remains small. A wheelchair symbol in a tourist brochure may be open to a variety of interpretations when it comes to accessibility.

Left **Bruges has many hotels of charm and character** Right **Bed-and-breakfast accomodation**

⁰⁰10 Accommodation Tips

1 Internet Information
There is a great deal of information about hotels, facilities and prices on the internet. Most hotels have their own websites, with links for enquiries and bookings.

2 How to Book
You can book by fax, internet or telephone (almost all reception staff speak English). Many hotels require security for a booking, such as a credit card number. The city tourist office *(see p112)* can also help you to find a room.

3 The Star System
The official star system for rating hotels is based more on facilities than on things that really make a difference, such as decor, tranquillity and quality of service. Two-star hotels may actually be more rewarding and agreeable than five-star ones. Le Dixseptième in Brussels *(see p125)* must rank among the most delightful hotels in the world, but it only has four stars, not five.

4 Weekend Rates
Many hotels offer weekend rates (Fri–Sun and public holidays), which are far cheaper that the standard "rack rate". In Brussels, the cheap rate may also cover every day in July and August, and through much of December to

mid-January. Many hotels also offer special rates if you stay several nights.

5 High and Low Seasons
Hotels prices reflect the predicted ebb and flow of business and holiday trade. Summer is busy in Bruges, but less so in Brussels, Antwerp or the university city of Ghent.

6 Hotels of Charm
For small hotels that are very comfortable and full of character, Bruges is way ahead of the other cities. In Antwerp and Ghent, such hotels are scarce; exceptions include the Flandria *(see p130)* and Matelote *(p131)*. Brussels has more to offer *(see p125)*.

7 Business Hotels
The hotel industry in Belgium is run with professionalism at all levels. In the business sector, pricing is highly competitive; the more you pay, the more you get – in terms of the facilities, at least.

8 Breakfast
Check whether breakfast is included in the price quoted – it can cost €15 a head or more if you pay separately. A hotel breakfast usually consists of a buffet, with cereals, croissants, cold meats and cheese, fruit, yogurts and jams, juices, and sometimes bacon and eggs.

9 Bed and Breakfa[st]
Private citizens in t[he] cities are, in increasing numbers, opening thei[r] homes for bed-and-breakfast accommodati[on] Some of these are delightful historic hous[es] right in the centre. The[y] are good value for mon[ey] – around €55–€95 for a double room, per night and the best tend to b[e] booked up months in advance. You can find many of the properties on the Internet. Tourist offices can also provid[e] listings and contacts *(and see panel below)*

10 Camping and Caravanning
A cheap option, at und[er] €20 per family per nig[ht] is to stay at one of Belgium's efficiently r[un] camping and caravann[ing] sites. Needless to say, they are not near the centres. Tourist offices will have details.

Bed-and-Breakfa[st] Accommodation

Bed & Brussels
02 646 07 37
• www.bnb-brussels.b[e]

Taxistop
070 222 292
• www.taxistop.be

Belsud
070 221 021
• www.belsud.be

Guild of Guesthous[es] in Gent
• www.bedandbreak-fast-gent.be

Fixed-price menus Right **Restaurant bills usually include service**

Eating and Drinking Tips

The Language of Food
nch was traditionally language of menus, ecially in the smarter aurants. Today, in Flemish cities, Dutch lead, followed by lish, perhaps with no nch at all. But it is to find a restaurant n no one to explain dishes in exquisite ail -- in whatever uage suits you best.

Follow the Locals
The Belgians love ng out, and they want d food at good prices. restaurant is not up scratch, they simply 't go there. If their ourite restaurant goes ugh a bad patch, they ert it. So choose the aurants that are full oca's (not hard to tell rt from the tourists).

Make a Reservation
d restaurants are y every day of the ek. If you set your rt on going to a icular one, be sure to ke a booking – easy ugh to do over the phone. If you change r mind, be sure to cel the reservation.

Fixed-price Menus
Special two- or three-rse menus offered at ted price, which often nge on a daily basis, be extremely good e. It's not simply a stion of price; the

chefs may have found ingredients at the market that took their fancy, and will be concentrating extra creative talents on them.

Vegetarians
Belgium is essentially a carnivorous and fish-loving nation, but most restaurants provide vegetarian options. There are also some dedicated vegetarian restaurants in all the cities, where chefs apply characteristic Belgian flare to their dishes. Tourist offices have listings.

Bloody, Rare and Well-done
Belgians like their beef fairly rare. If you ask for a medium-rare steak, it is likely to be more rare than medium. The beef's quality usually justifies light cooking, but if you want your meat well done, insist on it, and ignore raised eyebrows. Lamb is also served rare; if you don't like it that way, ask for it to be well done when you order.

Raw Meat, Raw Oysters
In certain dishes, beef is served raw. This applies to *Filet Américain (see p56)* and the widely adopted Italian dish *carpaccio*. Fish is served raw in the Japanese-influenced fusion dishes, and in salmon or tuna *carpaccio*. Oysters are likewise eaten raw.

Bills, Tax and Tipping
Value-added tax (TVA/BTW) at 21 per cent and a service charge of 16 per cent can add a lot to a restaurant bill, but both are usually included in the prices quoted in the menu. If you are not sure, don't be afraid to ask. If service is not included, you can add 10 per cent; if it is, you can add a small cash tip, but this is optional.

Eating with Children
Eating out is often a family event in Belgium; lunch can last half the afternoon. Children get used to this from an early age and may develop surprisingly sophisticated tastes. As a result, children are almost always welcomed in restaurants, and restaurateurs will go out of their way to satisfy their eating and drinking preferences. Children are also allowed into most cafés and bars.

Beer Strength
Belgian beers are, on average, somewhat stronger than their equivalents in Britain and the USA, and range from about 5% to 12% alcohol by volume. Since beers are served in fairly small quantities, the effect can be deceptive – until you stand up. It may need a bit of practice to get the measure of this.

For more on Belgian food **See pp56–7**

Left **Selection of beers** Right **Supermarket counter**

10 Shopping Tips

1 Tax Refunds
Visitors from outside the EU can reclaim most sales tax (TVA/BWT) on purchases above a minimum value of €175 from any one shop. Look for shops with the Tax-free Shopping sign. With sales tax at 21 per cent, this means a large saving on items of high value. You must obtain a "Tax-free Shopping Cheque" from the shop, and you can claim your refund at the Tax-free offices at Zavantem Airport. For more information, see www.globalrefund.com.

2 Customs Allowances
Residents of the EU face few limits on taking goods out of Belgium, but some restrictions apply to meat products, plants and, of course, weapons and narcotics. Alcohol and tobacco must be for personal use only; UK guidelines for maximum quantities in this respect are 10 litres of spirits, 800 cigarettes, 90 litres of wine, and 110 litres of beer. Non-EU visitors returning home are subject to far more restrictive limits on alcohol and tobacco.

3 Opening Hours
As a general rule, shops are open from 10am to 6pm; small shops such as bakeries and newsagents may open earlier. Some shops close for lunch but stay open later in the evening. On Sundays, larger shops and supermarkets close, but pâtisseries, chocolate shops, delicatessens and tourist shops are likely to remain open. Some shops stay open late on one night of the week, but none of the cites has a general late-night-shopping day.

4 Supermarkets
Many goods worth taking home – Trappist beers, Stella Artois lager, Côte d'Or chocolates – are found in supermarkets. The larger markets, such as those of the Delhaize chain, tend to be in the suburbs, but they also have mini stores in town.

5 Shopping Malls
All the cities have covered shopping malls (see pp 71, 90, 98 and 107), which are home to up-market boutiques and clothing chains.

6 Buying Chocolates
One of the great things about good-quality Belgian filled chocolates, or pralines, is that they contain fresh cream – which means they have a limited shelf-life. If you refrigerate them, however, they should be fine for about three weeks.

7 Beer and Wine
Belgian beer is remarkably good value, given its quality. There are specialist beer shops, but most of the better-known beers can be bought in ordinary food shops and supermarkets. The Belgians tend to drink French wine, and shop prices for wine are similar to French prices.

8 Genuine Lace
Genuine, hand-made lace is expensive. To ensure you are getting the real thing, insist on certificate of authentic (see p54).

9 Fashion
The city centres are packed with all sorts of clothes shops. Many items are imported, but the prices may still see good value. Belgium is also famous for its home-grown designer. Antwerp is the fashion design centre and has throng of shops that reflect this (see p107), but the clothes of the designers can be found in outlets elsewhere. There are also several respected Belgian labels (such as Olivier Strelli and Rue Blanche), with shops in most cities.

10 Books in English
All the cities have plenty of bookshops; the best offer many books English, including novel and guidebooks. Bruss has several specialist English-language book shops, including a branch of Waterstone's. ⊗ Boulevard Adolphe Ma 71–75 • Map C1

t Most museums and galleries are closed on Monday **Right** Pedestrian crossing

10 Things to Avoid

The Fast Lane
Do not be tempted imitate Belgian drivers motorway fast lanes. ey tend to drive nose--tail at top speed, as if e concept of "stopping stance" had gone out fashion.

Pedestrian Crossings
ell, you shouldn't *avoid* destrian crossings – t treat them with care. e law obliging drivers stop for pedestrians aiting to cross the road as introduced only in 96. Previously, drivers uld tend to ignore destrian crossings less someone actually alked in front of them. me drivers still seem follow this rule; others op punctiliously.

Priorité de Droite
In the past, traffic ming in from the right d priority, known as *iorité de droite*. Road arkings now indicate at priority belongs to affic on the main road, d that traffic joining a ain road must give way. ut vestiges of *priorité e droite* survive, notably suburban streets in russels, so keep an eye ut for road markings d traffic approaching om your right.

Drinking and Driving
rinking-and-driving is egal. One alcoholic ink, and you'll probably be just within the limit; two drinks and you may be over the limit – and, if stopped by police, liable to hefty penalties.

Driving into Bruges
Bruges does all it can to encourage you to park in one of the big car parks on the periphery of the city. The best solution is to go along with this, and walk the 1 km (half a mile) from the car parks to the city centre. However, it is possible to drive to your hotel and, indeed, to park close to the city centre, especially outside of the summer high season.

Mosquitoes
The canals of Bruges (and, to a lesser extent, those of Ghent) have always been a breeding ground for mosquitoes. This can be a nuisance in summer, so don't forget your insect repellent. If you fear that mosquitoes will bother you, choose an air-conditioned hotel, where you can keep the windows shut.

Getting Caught Short
Where there are public toilets in the cities, they are usually well run by caretakers, who ask for a contribution of about €0.30 for use of the facilities. Alternatively, use bar or café toilets – but, if you do so, behave like a customer and buy a drink or a coffee.

High Season in Bruges
Bruges is very busy in summer. Tour coaches arrive in droves, and release their throngs at car parks in the south-west of the city to pour into the streets leading to the centre. One way of dealing with this is to stay several days, so you can see the city in its more tranquil moments. Another is to explore the quieter areas – just about anywhere but the south-west. Still another is to come at a different time of year (but Bruges can be busy year-round).

Visiting Museums on Mondays
Monday is the day of rest for just about all the major museums and galleries – so it's a good day for walking, shopping, visiting churches, or whatever else takes your fancy.

Tourist Restaurants
You can spot them a mile off: plastic-coated menus printed in at least four languages; waiters who solicit your custom at the door; an entirely foreign clientèle; and restaurant terraces that occupy the most desirable locations in the city centre. Don't be tempted. The food in tourist restaurants is generally mediocre and poor value. Hunt a little further afield, or ask a local where to eat. The effort will be repaid.

It's almost impossible to eat badly in Belgium, but eating well may take a little research.

Left **International papers on a news stand** Right **Post office**

Banking & Communications

1 Changing Money
Belgium's currency is the Euro. Notes of other currencies and travellers' cheques can be changed or cashed at a bank or at one of the specialist exchange bureaus. To check whether or not you are getting a good deal, look at both the rate of exchange offered and the commission charged.

2 Banking Hours
Banks are generally open Mon–Fri 9am–1pm (or 9:30am–noon) and 2–4pm, but some larger branches do not close for lunch. Some banks open on Saturday mornings. The exchange bureaus have longer opening hours, and may be open through the weekend.

3 ATMs
Bank and credit cards can be used to draw cash from an ATM (Automatic Teller Machine). Before travelling, check with the bank or card issuer that your card is compatible with the systems used in Belgium (these include Cirrus, Maestro, Plus and Star). And make sure you know your PIN number.

4 Credit and Debit Cards
Most major credit and debit cards are accepted in Belgium. Restaurants almost always accept card payment, but check before you eat. A few of the smallest hotels accept only cash.

5 Travellers' Cheques
Travellers' cheques are a useful backup in case your cards get lost or stolen, or fail to work. They can be exchanged for cash, or – especially if they are in Euros – *used* as cash in certain circumstances.

6 Public Telephones
Mobile phones have made public pay-phones virtually redundant – but they still exist, operated by the former state company Belgacom, and can be used to make calls abroad. Public telephones operate with coins, or with Belgacom cards purchased from newsagents, ticket offices and post offices.

7 Post Offices
Post offices are generally open Mon–Fri 9am–5pm. You can buy stamps there and ascertain postage rates for heavier items. The main post offices in each city have poste restante facilities, and some offer fax services. Stamps are also available from some tobacconists, newsagents and shops selling postcards.

8 Internet
Many of the more business-oriented and up-market hotels have internet facilities. All the cities have cybercafés, many of them excellent.
🌐 www.cybercafes.com

9 Newspapers
The Belgian press is split across the language divide. The main French-language papers are *Le Soir*, *La Libre Belgique* and *La Dernière Heure*; the Dutch-speakers have *Het Laatste Nieuws*, *De Standaard* and *De Morgen*. English-language newspapers are, as in any other international city, widely available at news stands and in book shops. Brussels also has its own excellent English language weekly magazine called *The Bulletin*, offering a round up and analysis of local events, news stories and issues, as well as copious listings pages.

10 Television
Like their news-papers, Belgian television is split across the language divide, and cable brings in a wide choice of channels from all over Europe and the USA. Almost all hotel rooms have televisions.

Telephone codes

Belgian country code
+ 32 (drop the first 0 of the area code)

City area codes
Antwerp: (0)3
Bruges: (0)50
Brussels: (0)2
Ghent: (0)9

Dialling from Belgium
Britain: 00 44
USA/Canada: 00 1

  English is now widely spoken in all four of the cities covered in this book.

Pharmacy Right **Police officer giving directions**

Security and Health

Emergencies
The Belgians have a
well-developed sense of
community spirit, so if
you are unlucky enough
to face an emergency,
the chances are that you
will receive sympathetic
and effective help. The
emergency services are
as efficient and reliable
as any in Europe. ⊗ *Police:*
101 • Fire/accident/ ambu-
lance: 100 • Anti-poisoning
centre: 070 245 245

Travel Insurance
Take out travel and
health insurance when
you book your trip. This
will allow you to claim
compensation if you have
to cancel, are delayed,
or lose your possessions.
It also covers medical
costs in case of illness or
accident. British citizens
can take advantage of
reciprocal EU medical
agreements as long as
they carry a completed
E111 form, under which
80 per cent of specified
costs can be reclaimed.
You usually have to pay
for medical treatment
in the first instance and
claim costs later, for
which you will need
proper receipts.

Doctors
If you suffer an
accident or illness, you
might be treated by a GP,
or at one of the city
hospitals. Ask locally
about how best to
access these services;
for example, hotels have
lists of duty doctors.

Dentists
Belgian dentists
are generally of a high
standard. Ask locally
about how to access the
services of a duty dentist.

Hospitals
Belgium has a
tradition of hospital care
dating back to medieval
times. Most hospitals
have been rehoused in
modern buildings located
in spacious grounds and on
the periphery of the cities.
They rank among the
best in Europe.

Pharmacies
Pharmacists are
highly trained, and their
shops are often models
of clinical efficiency. To
many Belgians, the
pharmacist is the first
port of call for treatment
of minor ailments. But
pharmacists know the
limits of their jurisdiction,
and will refer you to a
doctor if necessary. Each
commune has a rota of
late-night pharmacies.

Breakdowns and Motoring Accidents
If you take your car to
Belgium, make sure you
have full breakdown cover.
If you don't, recovery
costs and, worse still,
the repatriation of your
vehicle, can cost a small
fortune. Breakdown
services are offered by
the two main Belgian
motoring organizations:
Touring and VAB.

⊗ *Touring: 070 34 47 77.*
www.touring.be • VAB:
070 344 666. www.
vab.be

Crime
Belgian cities are
not notably dangerous or
crime-ridden places, but
there is a fair amount of
pick-pocketing, theft, and
even car-jacking. If you
remain alert and exercise
the same precautions
as you would in any
other western city, the
chances are that you will
come through unscathed.
If you are the victim of a
crime, report it to the
police – within 24 hours
in the case of theft – if
you wish to claim
insurance. Many police
officers speak English,
and you are likely to get
a professional response.

Embassies
In extreme cases –
for instance, if you feel
you have been unfairly
treated by the police –
you might wish to contact
your country's embassy.
⊗ *UK: Rue d'Arlon 85,*
1040 Brussels (Etterbeek).
Map F4. 02 287 62 11 •
US: Blvd du Régent 27,
1000 Brussels. Map E3.
02 508 21 11

Identity
You are obliged by
law to carry an identity
document (e.g. passport)
at all times. The police
are entitled to ask you to
produce this for inspec-
tion, but they cannot
take it away from you.

Left **Astoria** Right **Radisson SAS Hotel**

Brussels Hotels: Top of the Range

1 Métropole
Brussels' best-known hotel is a glittering *belle époque* building updated to top modern standards. Centrally located, not far from Place Ste-Catherine and St-Géry. Ⓢ *Place de Brouckère 31, 1000 BRU • Map C2 • 02 217 23 00 • www.metropolehotel.com • €€€€€*

2 Astoria
With its palatial lobby and spectacular public rooms, the Astoria looks 18th-century, but was built in 1909. It stands in the Upper Town, near the Royal Palace. Churchill and Eisenhower stayed here. Ⓢ *Rue Royale 103, 1000 BRU • Map D2 • 02 227 05 05 • €€€€€*

3 Amigo
Smart, comfortable and efficient, the Amigo occupies the site of a 16th-century city prison near the Grand Place. Its interior is in Spanish Renaissance style. Ⓢ *Rue de l'Amigo 1–3, 1000 BRU • Map B3 • 02 547 47 47 • www.hotelamigo.com • €€€€€*

4 NH Hotel du Grand Sablon
The location of this hotel, overlooking the pretty Place du Grand Sablon, is one of its main selling points – that, and the fact that it offers the first-class facilities of this stylish Italian chain. Elegant, modern and comfortable. At weekends, room rates drop by 50 per cent. Ⓢ *Rue Bodenbroeck 2–4, 1000 BRU • Map C4 • 02 518 11 00 • www.nh-hotels.com • €€€€€*

5 Brussels Marriott Hotel
Impressive addition to the Marriott chain, located near the Bourse and the Grand Place, ideally located for business, shopping and leisure. Ⓢ *Rue Auguste Orts 3–7, 1000 BRU • Map B2 • 02 516 90 90 • www.marriott.com • €€€€*

6 Silken Berlaymont
Close to the heart of European government and the Cinquantenaire, this hotel is favoured by diplomats, politicians and journalists. They make full use of its state-of-the-art communication systems, fitness centre, Turkish baths and sauna. Ⓢ *Boulevard Charlemagne 11–19, 1000 BRU • Map G3 • 02 231 09 09 • www.hotelsilkenberlaymont.com • €€€€€*

7 Royal Windsor
Equidistant from the Grand Place and the Musées Royaux des Beaux-Arts, this elegant and sumptuous hotel features a series of "Fashion Rooms" designed by Belgian fashion designers. Ⓢ *Rue Duquesnoy 5, 1000 BRU • Map C3 • 02 505 55 55 • www.royalwindsorbrussels.com • €€€€€*

8 Radisson SAS Royal Hotel
The foyer is breathtaking – a towering atrium, with tropical plants and fountains filling its base and glass-fronted lifts rising into the firmament. Managed with stylish efficiency, the hotel has a renowned restaurant, the Sea Grill *(see p74)*. Ⓢ *Rue Fossé-aux-Loups 4, 1000 BRU • Map C2 • 02 219 28 28 • www.radissonsas.com • €€€€€*

9 Conrad International
South-west of the "Pentagon" delineating the old city, the Conrad lies close to the prime shopping area around the Place Louise. A polished and comfortable modern hotel, offering huge bedrooms, and two well-respected restaurants. Ⓢ *Avenue Louise 71, 1050 BRU • Map C6 • 02 542 42 42 • www.conradhotels.com • €€€€€*

10 The Dominican
This luxurious hotel cannot be beaten for location, right behind Théâtre Royal de la Monnaie and within walking distance of the Grand Place. Award-winning architects have created private courtyard over which the rooms look, and a very public and sumptuous Grand Lounge. Ⓢ *Rue Léopold 9, 1000 BRU • Map C2 • 02 203 08 087 • www.thedominican.be • €€€€€*

Price Categories

For a standard, double room per night (with breakfast if included), taxes and extra charges.	
€	under €60
€€	€60–€100
€€€	€100–€175
€€€€	€175–€250
€€€€€	over €250

Plaza

Brussels: Hotels of Character

Le Dixseptième
There is no other place quite like this in Brussels: an utterly charming and fascinating small hotel in the late-17th-century residence of the Spanish ambassador. It has a number of suites named after Belgian artists – ingeniously devised beneath the roof beams, and furnished with a mixture of antique charm and modern flair.
◊ *Rue de la Madeleine 25, 1000 BRU • Map C3 • 02 517 17 17 • www.ledixseptieme.be • €€€€*

Manos Premier
This spectacularly styled hotel feels like a large and elegant private home. Many of the rooms are characterful suites, some with private roof terraces. Located south of the city centre, outside the Pentagon.
◊ *Chaussée de Charleroi 100–106, 1060 BRU (Saint-Gilles) • Map C6 • 02 537 96 82 • www.manoshotel.com /premier • €€€€€*

Le Plaza
You feel a bit like a guest of Louis XVI in the palatial foyer and public rooms of this grand hotel, with its stucco, gilt, and lavish ceiling paintings. The rooms maintain the same high standard of spacious comfort. ◊ *Boulevard Adolphe Max 118–26, 1000 BRU • Map C1 • 02 278 01 00 • www.leplaza-brussels. com • €€€€*

Warwick Barsey Hotel
Located at the southern end of Avenue Louise, this hotel has been redecorated by French designer Jacques Garcia in an opulent Edwardian style. The rooms exude a sense of luxurious, silky comfort. ◊ *Avenue Louise 381–3, 1050 BRU • 02 649 98 00 • www.warwickbarsey.com • €€€€€*

Stanhope
This elegant hotel, close to the Royal Palace, is decorated in a modern interpretation of British country-house style. Attractive weekend rates. ◊ *Square de Meeus 4, 1000 BRU • Map E5 • 02 506 91 11 • www. thonhotels.be • €€€€*

Comfort Art Hotel Siru
Each of the 101 rooms has been decorated by a modern Belgian artist, to varying and unusual effect. Just south of the Gare du Nord, within easy walking distance of the city centre. ◊ *Place Rogier 1, 1210 BRU (Saint-Josse-ten-Noode) • Map C1 • 02 203 35 80 • www. comforthotelsiru.com • €€€€€*

Hilton Brussels City
Facing the Comfort Art Hotel Siru, on the other side of Place Rogier, this hotel is a modern interpretation of Art Deco – all chrome and sensual wooden surfaces, and satisfying geometric surprises. ◊ *Place Rogier 20, 1210 BRU (Saint-Josse-ten-Noode) • Map C1 • 02 203 31 25 • www.hilton.com • €€€€€*

Hotel Bloom!
A functional and modern hotel; all-white rooms each with a fresco painted by a young European artist. Located behind the botanical gardens with easy access to the Gare du Nord and the city centre. ◊ *Rue Royale 250, 1210 BRU • Map D1 • 02 220 66 11 • www. hotelbloom.com • €€€€*

The White Hotel
Another hotel featuring rooms individually decorated by young artists. The hotel's welcome pack includes a useful list of the best places to visit in Brussels. Bicycle and scooter hire available. ◊ *Avenue Louise 212, 1050 BRU • Map C6 • 02 644 29 29 • www. thewhitehotel.be • €€€*

A La Grande Cloche
On a quiet square close to the Grand Place this attractive hotel offers exceptionally good value. Conveniently located opposite the famous Comme Chez Soi restaurant *(see p74)*, it is perfect for gourmands. ◊ *Place Rouppe 10, 1000 BRU • Map B4 • 02 512 61 40 • www.hotelgrande cloche.com • €€*

Left **Le Châtelain** Right **NH Atlanta**

⟨Top⟩10 Brussels Hotels: Business & Budget

1 Novotel Brussels Centre – Tour Noire

This efficient business hotel incorporates an "aquatic health centre" and the Tour Noire, a rare surviving watchtower of the 12th-century city walls. ✆ *Rue de la Vierge Noire 32, 1000 BRU • Map B2 • 02 505 50 50 • www.novotel.com • €€€*

2 Vendôme Marivaux

A simple but satisfactory business hotel, the Vendôme is within easy walking distance of the Grand Place. ✆ *Boulevard Adolphe Max 98, 1000 BRU • Map C1 • 02 227 03 00 • www.hotel-vendome.be • €€€€*

3 NH Atlanta

This stylish, modern hotel is run with charm and professionalism. Special features include spacious marbled bathrooms and a rooftop breakfast room. ✆ *Boulevard Adolphe Max 7, 1000 BRU • Map C2 • 02 217 01 20 • www.nh-hotels.com • €€€€*

4 Atlas

A well-run, modern hotel not far from Place Sainte-Catherine, Place Saint-Géry and the Grand Place, the Atlas offers off-peak bargains on its website. ✆ *Rue du Vieux Marché aux Grains 30, 1000 BRU • Map B2 • 02 502 60 06 • www.atlas-hotel.be • €€€€*

5 Citadines

At Citadines, you can rent a studio or an apartment with kitchen and living areas. The flats are available for single nights, but are better value for longer stays. Reasonably priced and centrally located in the Place Sainte-Catherine area. ✆ *Quai au Bois à Brûler 51, 1000 BRU • Map B1 • 02 221 14 11 • www.citadines.com • €€*

6 Le Châtelain

Although its 1000 post code suggests central Brussels, this hotel is halfway along Avenue Louise, close to the Musée Horta. Its mixture of elegance and efficiency is reflected in its room prices. ✆ *Rue du Châtelain 17, 1000 BRU • 02 646 00 55 • www.le-chatelain.com • €€€€€*

7 Noga

This well-managed small hotel has a loyal following. Decorated in a mixture of modern and antique styles, it has a picturesque charm, and is centrally located in the tranquil Béguinage district, close to Place Sainte-Catherine. ✆ *Rue du Béguinage 38, 1000 BRU • Map B1 • 02 218 67 63 • www.nogahotel.com • €€*

8 George V

A small, friendly hotel in a 19th-century *maison de maître*, with touches of old-world English charm, the George V lies to the west of the Grand Place, close to the lively cafés and bars of Place Saint-Géry. ✆ *Rue t'Kint 23, 1000 BRU • Map A3 • 02 513 50 93 • www.george5.com • €€*

9 Brussels Welcome Hotel

Located close to the Grand Place, this friendly informal hotel features geographical theme to each of its 15 remarkable rooms. Choose your imaginary destination for the night – Congo, Cuba, India or Istanbul. The neighbourhood has a bohemian feel and is close to the city's trendier shops. ✆ *Quai au bois à Brûler 23, 1000 BRU • Map B1 • 02 219 95 46 • www.brusselshotel.travel • €€*

10 Sleep Well Youth Hotel

Some aspects of this centrally located budget hotel resemble a youth hostel (shared bathrooms; rooms inaccessible 11am–3pm), but it offers clean, modern accommodation and represents extremely good value, especially for families or groups. A newer, more up-market annexe called the New Sleep Well has en-suite bathrooms and rooms at three times the price of the older ones. ✆ *Rue du Damier 23, 1000 BRU • Map C1 • 02 218 50 50 • www.sleepwell.be • €*

Price Categories

For a standard, double room per night (with breakfast if included), taxes and extra charges.

€ under €60
€€ €60–€100
€€€ €100–€175
€€€€ €175–€250
€€€€€ over €250

artin's Orangerie

10 Bruges Hotels: Luxury

1 Die Swaene
A small hotel in a row 15th-century houses verlooking the canal, Die waene is right in the entre of Bruges, close the Burg. Four-poster eds, swimming pool nd an excellent restau- nt. ◈ *Steenhouwersdijk 1 • Map L4 • 050 34 27 98 • www.dieswaene-hotel. om • €€€€*

2 Martin's Orangerie
This delightful hotel a 15th-century building as a gorgeous panelled reakfast room and unge with a terrace verlooking the Den ijver canal. The hotel xudes character and harm. ◈ *Kartuizerinnen- traat 10 • Map K4 • 050 4 16 49 • www.martins otels.com • €€€€*

3 De Tuilerieën
The sister hotel of e Orangerie, near the roeningemuseum, has sense of refined 18th- entury urban elegance and a swimming pool. ◈ *Dijver 7 • Map L4 • 050 4 36 91 • www.hotel ilerieen.com • €€€€€*

4 Pandhotel
This luxurious hotel, a fine 18th-century wn house, has made pecial efforts to live up its "romantic" label. is beautifully decorated a very comfortable, eeply upholstered style, ith canopied beds. lose to the Burg in a etty tree-lined street.

◈ *Pandreitje 16 • Map L4 • 050 34 06 66 • www. pandhotel.com • €€€*

5 Kempinski Dukes' Palace
Deserving of its 5 stars, this former ducal palace is up to the usual Kempiski decorative standard, but the spa pool, art gallery and chapel make it some- thing extra special. The Manuscript restaurant serves a great breakfast. The bar is not cheap but locals seem to think it's worth it. ◈ *Prinsenhof 8 • Map K4 • 050 44 78 88 • www.kempinski-bruges. com • €€€€€*

6 Relais Oud Huis Amsterdam
A group of 17th-century mansion houses lining the Spiegelrei canal, north of the Markt, is the setting for one of Bruges' best- loved hotels. Rooms have handsome antiques, and everything is styled with a casual elegance, giving the hotel a relaxed and distinctive charm, which is reflected in the man- agement style. ◈ *Spiegel- rei 3 • Map L3 • 050 34 18 10 • www.oha.be • €€€€*

7 NH Brugge
Of the many hotels that line the Zand – a large open space in the west – this is probably the best. Rooms are comfortable, and the indoor swimming pool is a bonus. ◈ *Boeveriestraat 2 • Map J5 • 050 44 97 11 • www. nh-hotels.com • €€€€*

8 De Castillion
Occupying a 17th- century bishop's residence in the west of the city, this comfortable hotel has imaginatively decorated bedrooms and bathrooms. The high standard of the rooms is matched by the hotel's sumptuous restaurant, Le Manoir Quatre Saisons. ◈ *Heilige Geeststraat 1 • Map K4 • 050 34 30 01 • www. castillion.be • €€€€*

9 Crowne Plaza Hotel
You could not get more central than this if you tried: the Crowne Plaza overlooks the Burg at the very heart of Bruges. An efficiently run, modern establishment, it also incorporates some historic remains: the excavated foundations of the medieval church of St Donatian. The hotel has an indoor swimming pool and its own car park. ◈ *Burg 10 • Map L4 • 050 44 68 44 • www. crowneplaza.com/bruggebel • €€€€€*

10 De' Medici
This smart, modern hotel, overlooking the canal in the quieter, east- ern part of town, is a member of the Golden Tulip group. Unusually, it has a Japanese restau- rant. It also has a gym, a sauna and Turkish baths. ◈ *Potterierei 15 • Map L2 • 050 33 98 33 • www. hoteldemedici.com • €€€€*

Streetsmart

Left **Navarra** Right **Jan Brito**

Bruges Hotels: Mid-range

Navarra
The former trading house of the merchants of Navarre is now a hotel of unusual elegance sited to the north of the Markt. A member of the Best Western group, it offers a high standard of service and comfort, including a fitness centre and swimming pool. Ⓢ Sint-Jakobsstraat 41 • Map K3 • 050 34 05 61 • www.hotelnavarra.com • €€€

Adornes
The Adornes is set in a renovated set of 16th- to 18th-century mansions overlooking the canal in the quieter, eastern part of the city, yet within walking distance of the centre. The decor, with its exposed beams, has the fresh-faced appeal of rustic charm. Guests have free use of bicycles. Ⓢ Sint-Annarei 26 • Map L3 • 050 34 13 36 • www.adornes.be • €€€

Prinsenhof
Part of the Relais du Silence group, this neat little hotel is tucked away down a side street in the west of the city, in an area once occupied by the splendid palace of the dukes of Burgundy. Something of the dukes' grand style pervades the decor – on a smaller scale, of course. Ⓢ Ontvangersstraat 9 • Map K4 • 050 34 26 90 • www.prinsenhof.be • €€€

Walburg
A grand 19th-century mansion, beautifully restored to a state of cool and spacious elegance. The Walburg exudes style and opulence, with a three-floor atrium, a marble staircase and Louis XVI-style furniture. Ⓢ Boomgaardstraat 13–15 • Map L3 • 050 34 94 14 • www.hotelwalburg.be • €€€€

Hotel Jacobs
This good-value and intimate hotel is located in the quiet Saint-Gillis neighbourhood. Run by the affable Gentile family, it offers clean, comfortable public areas and cosy bedrooms. Within walking distance to the main shops, restaurants and museums. Ⓢ Baliestraat 1 • Map L2 • 050 33 98 31 • www.hoteljacobs.be • €€

Egmond
The Egmond feels like a world apart, set in its own little tree-shaded park next to the Minne-water, in the south of the town. The façades and manor-house style give it a neo-baronial air. Ⓢ Minnewater 15 • Map K6 • 050 34 14 45 • www.egmond.be • €€€

Ibis Brugge Centrum
In this hotel, you'll find the no-frills, straight-forward efficiency of the Ibis chain. It may lack historic charm, but it satisfies essential requirements, and is conveniently located. Ⓢ Katelijnestraat 65a • Map L5 • 050 33 75 75 • www.ibishotel.com • €€

Heritage
A smart, comfortabl[e] hotel in a 19th-century mansion, located in the old merchant quarter to the north of the Markt. [I]t boasts a spa and fitness room in the 14th-centur[y] cellar, and a sun deck o[n] the roof. Ⓢ Niklaas Desparsstraat 11 • Map K[.] • 050 44 44 44 • www.hotel-heritage.be • €€€

Parkhotel
One of the larger hotels on the Zand, the Parkhotel is well-run, wi[th] elegant, easy-on-the-eye[ ]decor and efficient service. It overlooks the Zand, the spacious market square to the west o[f] the city, and is 10 minutes from the city centr[e.] Ⓢ Vrijdagmarkt 5 • Map J[.] • 050 33 33 64 • www.parkhotel-brugge.be • €€€

Jan Brito
Centrally located, between the Burg and the Koningin Astridpark, the Jan Brito occupies a[n] attractive 16th-century building with a step-gabled, brick façade. The charming public rooms are decorated in Louis XVI style. There is a pre[t]ty garden. Ⓢ Freren Fonteinstraat 1 • Map L4 • 05[0] 33 06 01 • www.janbrito.com • €€€

Price Categories
For a standard, double room per night (with breakfast if included), taxes and extra charges.

€	under €60
€€	€60–€100
€€€	€100–€175
€€€€	€175–€250
€€€€€	over €250

10 Bruges Hotels: Budget

Botaniek
A small but attractive hotel, stacked vertically in the narrow footprint of an 18th-century mansion. The rooms are straightforward but pleasant, the public rooms attractive. Above all, the welcome is friendly and helpful. The location – close to the Koningin Astridpark – is conveniently central. Look out for special offers on their website. ✪ Waalsestraat 23 • Map K4 • 050 34 14 24 • www.botaniek.be • €€

Patritius
Given its prices, the Patritius occupies a surprisingly grand 19th-century mansion located to the north-east of the Markt. ✪ Ridderstraat 11 • Map L3 • 050 33 84 54 • www.hotelpatritius.be • €€

Ter Brughe
The area just north of the Augustijnenrei canal is a charming web of old streets. This well-run hotel occupies a 16th-century house overlooking the canal. The breakfast room is in the brick-vaulted cellar. ✪ Oost Gistelhof 2 • Map K3 • 050 34 03 24 • www.hotelterbrughe.com • €€€

Ter Duinen
This small hotel may seem a little out of the way in the north of the city, but the centre of Bruges is only a 15-minute walk away. The well-presented rooms are double-glazed and air-conditioned. The public rooms are stylish and welcoming. ✪ Langerei 52 • Map L2 • 050 33 04 37 • www.terduinenhotel.be • €€€

Lucca
The 18th-century Neo-Classical exterior conceals an even older interior, with a vaulted medieval cellar in which guests breakfast. This was once the lodge of the merchants of Lucca – with connections to Giovanni Arnolfini, the banker who features in Jan van Eyck's famous painting, The Arnolfini Marriage. The rooms are quaintly old-fashioned – a fact reflected in the attractive room price. ✪ Naaldenstraat 30 • Map K3 • 050 34 20 67 • www.hotellucca.be • €€

Ter Reien
Fetchingly perched beside the canal a little to the east of the Burg, Ter Reien is noted for the quality of its rooms, its service and, above all, its value for money. ✪ Langestraat 1 • Map L3 • 050 34 91 00 • www.hotelterreien.be • €€

De Pauw
This pretty, family-run hotel, with its weathered brick exterior draped with flowers, is located close to the old parish church of St Giles, in the quiet and historic northern part of town – but still just a 10-minute walk from the centre. The interior is styled like a private home, with a welcome to match. ✪ Sint-Gilliskerkhof 8 • Map L2 • 050 33 71 18 • www.hoteldepauw.be • €€

Passage
Interesting budget hotel with just 14 rooms, styled with exotic and Bohemian flair. It also has an adjacent "youth hotel", with cheaper prices. It is attached to the equally alluring Gran Kaffee de Passage (see p93). ✪ Dweerstraat 26 • Map K4 • 050 34 02 32 • www.passagebruges.com • €

Bauhaus Hotel
This "International Youth Hotel" is popular, energetic and friendly. Located in the east of the city, a 15-minute walk from the centre, it prides itself on its cheap accommodation, its well-priced restaurants and bar, and its cybercafé. ✪ Langestraat 135 • Map M3 • 050 34 10 93 • www.bauhaus.be • €

Charlie Rockets
This youth hotel is housed in a converted cinema, fronted by a big, raucous café-bar serving nachos and burgers to the beat of rock. Rooms are basic, but keenly priced – especially given the location, just to the east of the Burg. ✪ Hoogstraat 19 • Map L4 • 050 33 06 60 • www.charlierockets.com • €

Left **Hotel Harmony** Right **Poortackere Monasterium**

Ghent Hotels

Ghent River Hotel
This functional, modern hotel has 77 rooms occupying a converted 16th-century house and 19th-century factory. It is located on the bank of the River Leie close to the lively Vrijdagmarkt. A small brick pier means that this is the city's only hotel that can be accessed by boat. ✆ Waaistraat 5 • Map Q1 • 09 266 10 10 • www.ghent-river-hotel.be • €€€

Hotel Harmony
A stylish, family-run hotel located in Patershof, the oldest quarter of Ghent. The hotel features a courtyard swimming pool and a series of upscale rooms facing the canal; all have roof terraces with views over the city. ✆ Kraanlei 37 • Map Q1 • 09 324 26 80 • www.hotel-harmony.be • €€€

NH Gent Belfort
This chain certainly knows how to deliver style and comfort. The Belfort has all the facilities of a hotel of this rank, including a fitness room and sauna, and is very centrally located, opposite the Stadhuis. ✆ Hoogpoort 63 • Map Q2 • 09 233 33 31 • www.nh-hotels.com • €€€€€

Hotel de Flandre
Tucked behind the Korenlei quayside, this stylish town house has retained plenty of period detail in its public areas while its bedrooms are plainer but comfortable. ✆ Poel 1–2 • Map P2 • 09 266 06 00 • www.hoteldeflandre.be • €€€

Aparthotel Castelnou
A modern block in the east of the city, about 15 to 20 minutes' walk from Sint-Baafskathedraal, provides moderately priced rooms. The hotel is divided into apartments, as well as conventional rooms, all of which are available for one night or longer stays. It also has a restaurant, which, given its location, is useful. ✆ Kasteellaan 51 • 09 235 04 11 • www.castelnou.be • €€

Ibis Gent Centrum Kathedraal
Right in the centre of Ghent, overlooking Sint-Baafskathedraal, this is a well-run, modern and attractive member of the reliable Ibis chain. ✆ Limburgstraat 2 • Map Q2 • 09 233 00 00 • www.ibishotel.com • €€€

Ibis Gent Centrum Opera
This second Ibis hotel is located to the south of the city centre, about 10 minutes' walk from Sint-Baafskathedraal. Although somewhat functional, it is well-run and popular. If driving, be sure to ask for directions, as Ghent's one-way system is maddening and makes access to the hotel something of a challenge. ✆ Nederkouter 24–6 • Map P3 • 09 225 07 07 • www.ibishotel.com • €€€

Monasterium Poortackere
Here is an interesting experience: a hotel in a converted convent. An air of tranquillity pervades the (largely 19th-century) buildings and grounds. A special place, enhanced by a warm welcome and a relaxed atmosphere – and a convenient location just west of the city centre. ✆ Oude Houtlei 56 • Map P2 • 09 269 22 10 • www.poortackere.com • €€

Flandria
Tucked away in a quiet street to the east of Sint-Baafskathedraal is this fetching budget hotel. It is especially good value for families with three to five sharing. ✆ Barrestraat 3 • Map R2 • 09 223 06 26 • www.flandria-centrum.be • €

NH Ghent
A comfortable, modern hotel just as you would expect from the reliable NH chain. It lies in a rather remote location about 1.5 km (1 mile) from Sint-Baafskathedraal. ✆ Koning Albertlaan 121 • Map N5 • 09 222 60 65 • www.nh-hotels.com • €€€

Price Categories

For a standard,
double room per
night (with breakfast
if included), taxes
and extra charges.

€ under €60
€€ €60–€100
€€€ €100–€175
€€€€ €175–€250
€€€€€ over €250

Radisson SAS Park Lane

10 Antwerp Hotels

Julien
A contemporary hotel
with grey and white
interiors. Fashioned out
of two town houses
linked by a green patio, it
is located between Meir,
the main shopping area,
and the cathedral. ✆
Korte Nieuwstraat 24 • Map
T2 • 03 229 06 00 • www.
hotel-julien.com • €€€€

Radisson SAS Park Lane
As you would expect
from the name, the Rad-
isson SAS is a smart,
well-run, modern hotel. It
faces onto the Stadspark,
about 1.5 km (1 mile) to
the south-east of the
cathedral. Fitness suite.
Swimming pool. ✆ Van
Eycklei 34 • Map U3
• 03 285 85 85 • www.
radissonsas.com • €€€€

Hilton
Overlooking the
Groenplaats, right in the
middle of Antwerp, is the
extraordinary dome-
roofed palace built as the
Grand Bazar du Bon
Marché, a 1920s depart-
ment store. Part of it has
now been converted into
this top-class, stylish and
well-appointed Hilton
hotel. Most of the rooms
overlook a quiet inner
courtyard. ✆ Groenplaats
• Map T2 • 03 204 12 12
• www.hilton.com • €€€€€

Matelote
This converted town
house near the River
Scheldt offers nine
dazzlingly white rooms all

with minimalist decor
and modern facilities.
Breakfast is taken in the
neighbouring Gin-Fish
restaurant, which used to
be called De Matelote
(hence the name). ✆
Haarstraat 11A
• Map T2 • 03 201 88 00
• www.matelote.be • €€€

Theater Hotel
This modern hotel
lies in a convenient
location close to the
Rubenshuis, and is a
short walk from the
cathedral via some of
Antwerp's best shopping
streets. ✆ Arenbergstraat
30 • Map U2 • 03 203 54
10 • www. vhv-hotels.be
• €€€€

Antigone
A tidy, modern and
reasonably-priced hotel
overlooking the river (and
road), the Antigone is
conveniently placed for
the Grote Markt and
cathedral, as well as
some of the clubs, bars
and restaurants just
north of the city centre.
✆ Jordaenskaai 11–12
• Map T1 • 03 231 66 77 •
www.antigonehotel.be • €€

't Sandt
This hotel in an old
patrician mansion has
been elegantly kitted out
in a style you might call
"Neo-Rococo". All the
suites, including the
luxurious penthouse, are
set around a courtyard
garden. It lies just to the
west of the cathedral,
and close to the river.

✆ Zand 17 • Map T2 • 03
232 93 90 • www.hotel-
sandt.be • €€€

Radisson SAS Astrid Hotel
This is a large and well-
run hotel, close to the
Centraal Station, east of
the city centre. It offers
extensive conference
facilities, and is well
suited to the business
traveller. It has a fitness
suite and swimming
pool. ✆ Koningin Astrid-
plein 7 • Map V2 • 03 203
12 34 • www.radissonsas.
com • €€€€

Ibis Antwerpen Centrum
For shopping you can't
get much more central
than this 150-room
modern hotel with an
entrance just off Meir.
Bicycles can be hired
from the reception and
are an ideal way to
get around the city.
✆ Meistraat 39 • Map U2
• 03 231 88 30 • www.
ibishotel.com • €€

Scheldezicht
From its position
overlooking a little square
just to the south-west of
the cathedral, this
friendly, popular and
well-priced hotel has
views over the River
Scheldt. The hotel exudes
old-world but unstuffy
charm. Breakfast is
served in an oak-panelled
room. ✆ Sint-Jansvliet
10–12 • Map T2 • 03 231
66 02 • www.hotelschelde
zicht.be • €€

General Index

Acknowledgments

The Author

Antony Mason is the author of a number of guide books, including the Cadogan City Guides to *Bruges* and to *Brussels (with Bruges, Ghent and Antwerp)*. He is also the author of the volume on *The Belgians* in the humorous Xenophobe's Guides series – along with more than 50 other books on history, geography, exploration and art. He lives in London with his Belgian wife Myriam, and their son Lawrence.

For their help, deeply appreciated, the author would like to thank: Dawn Page, Ilse Van Steen, Anousjka Schmidt, Jean-Pierre Drubbel, Anne De Meerleer, Joke Dieryckx and Frank Deijnckens.

Produced by DP Services, a division of DUNCAN PETERSEN PUBLISHING LTD, 31 Ceylon Road, London W14 0PY

Project Editor Chris Barstow
Designer Janis Utton
Picture Researcher Lily Sellar
Indexer Hilary Bird

Fact Checker Dan Colwell
Main Photographer Anthony Souter
Additional Photography Demetrio Carrasco, Paul Kenward, David Murray, Jules Selmes

Illustrator chrisorr.com

Maps Dominic Beddow, Simonetta Giori (Draughtsman Ltd)

FOR DORLING KINDERSLEY
Publisher Douglas Amrine
Senior Art Editor Kate Poole
Senior Cartographic Editor Casper Morris
DTP Jason Little
Production Bethan Blase
Additional Editorial Assistance Emma Anacootee, Dan Colwell, Rhiannon Furbear, Carly Madden, Sam Merrell, Kate Molan, Adrian Mourby, Marianne Petrou, Simon Ryder, Sadie Smith

Picture Credits

Placement Key: t-top; tc-top centre; tl-top left; tr-top right; cla-centre left above; ca-centre above; cra-centre right above; cl-centre left; c-centre; cr-centre right; clb-centre left below; cb-centre below; crb-centre right below; bl-below left; bc-below centre; br-below right; b-bottom.

Every effort has been made to trace the copyright holders and we apologize in advance for any unintentional omissions. We would be pleased to insert the appropriate acknowledgements in any subsequent edition of this publication.

Works of art have been reproduced with the permission of the following copyright holders: *L Masques Singuliers* (1892) James Ensor ©DACS London 2008 13cra; *The Domain of Arnheim* Re Magritte ©ADAGP, Paris and DACS, London 2008 13cr; *Baigneuse* (1910) Léon Spilliaert ©DACS London 2006 15b, *Les Troncs Gris* Léon Spilliaert ©DACS, London 2006 34br; ©Hergé/Moulinsart 2003 21cb, 55bl; Sofa Kandissy ©Alessandro Medini 39b.

The publishers would like to thank the following individuals, companies and picture libraries for permission to reproduce their photographs:

AKG-IMAGES: Collection Schloss Ambras, Innsbruck/Erich Lessing, *Charles V* (1549) copy after Tizian 47 cr; Museum der Bildenden Künste Leipzig, *Die Grubenarbeiterrinnen* (1880) by Constantin Meunier 37 cr; Kunsthistorisches Museum, Vienna/Erich Lessing, *Philippe III le Bo (the Good), Duke of Burgundy* (c.1500) after a low original by Rogier van der Weyden (Roger de la Pasture); Antwerp Tourist Office: 53br, 53bl, 61 64-65c, 102tr, 103br, 104tl, 104cr, 105bl, 105cr, 106tl, 106tr.

BCB: Daniel Fouss 20–21c, 21tl.

BRIDGEMAN ART LIBRARY: Christies Images, London, *Self Portrait* by Peter Paul Rubens (1557 1640) 30-31c; Koninklijk Museum voor Schone Kunsten, Antwerp, *Pièta* (c.1629) by Sir Anthony van Dyck 37tl.

CAFÉ DU VAUDEVILLE: Jean Mart 72tr.

CH. BASTIN & J. EVRARD: 34tl, 44bc.

CITY OF BRUSSELS MUSEUM/MAISON DU ROI *The River Senne* by J.B. van Moer 11b.

CORBIS: 56tr; Archivo Iconografico, S.A, *The Ghent Altarpiece* (1432) by Hubert van Eyck Jan van Eyck (detail) 7crb, 36tr, 94tl, 26cb, 26br,

27cr, 27cb, 35br; Dave Bartruff 22cb; Michael
selle 82-83c; Owen Franken 55cr; E.O. Hoppé
r; Diego Lezama Orezzoli 32-33c; Sygma/John
selt 50tr; Sygma/Van Parys 48clb.

N DIJVER: 92tr.

VLAAMSE OPERA, GHENT: Kurt Van der Elst
r.

ENT TOURIST OFFICE: 26tl, 94tr, 95tr, 96cl, 97cr.

T BRUGS DIAMANTMUSEUM: 88tr.

TEL HARMONY: Bram Declercq 130tl.

FLANDERS FIELDS MUSEUM: 63tr.

NINKLIJK MUSEUM VOOR SCHONE KUNSTEN,
twerpen (België) 102tl.

CHÂTELAIN ALL SUITE HOTEL: Harshad B.ICKX
6tl.

ONARDO MEDIABANK: 131tl.

tub 2003: J. Lafont 40tr, 78tl.

ARTIN'S ORANGERIE: 127t.l

ARY EVANS PICTURE LIBRARY: 47cl.

USÉE D'IXELLES, BRUXELLES: Collection
linistère de la Communauté Française de Belgique,
es Troncs Gris by Léon Spillaert 34br ©DACS,
ondon 2006.

USÉE DES INSTRUMENTS DE MUSIQUE: 6cb,
6cla, 16-17c, 17t, 17cb, 17b, 38tr, 53tr.

USÉE DES SCIENCES NATURELLES: Photo-foto
scnb-kbin Th.Hubin 41br.

USÉES ROYAUX DES BEAUX-ARTS DE
BELGIQUE BRUXELLES – KONINKLIJKE MUSEA
VOOR SCHONE KUNSTEN VAN BELGIË: 14tr; photo
Speltdoorn, Death of Marat (1793) by Jacque-Louis
David 6cl, 13tc, Les Masques Singuliers (1892)
James Ensor ©DACS, London 2008 13cra, Pietà by
Rogier van der Weyden 12bra, The Domain of
Arnheim by René Magritte 13cr ©ADAGP, Paris and
DACS, London 2006, La Belle Captive (1965) by
Magritte 14tc; Marché d'oranges à Blidah (1898) by
Henri Evenepoel 15t, Baigneuse by Léon Spillaert

15b ©DACS 2006, Portrait de Laurent Froimont by
Rogier van der Weyden 36bl, Triptyque: Le Ruisseau
by Baron Léon Frederic 67bc; photo Cussac,
Episode des Journées de Septembre 1830 sur la
Place de l'Hôtel de Ville de Bruxelles (1835) by Baron
Gustaf Wappers 46tr, L'inhumation Precipité by
Antoine Wiertz 40bl, L'assomption de la Vierge by
Peter Paul Rubens 36tl, Dame en Bleu Devant une
Glace (1914) by Rik Wouters 34cl, Du Silence (1980)
Fernand Khnopff 13bl, La Chute d'Icare by Pieter
Bruegel I 12bc.

MUSÉE DAVID ET ALICE VAN BUUREN: 34tr.

NEIL SETCHFIELD: 4-5c, 58tl.

OFFICE DE PROMOTION DU TOURISME
WALLONIE: 76tl, 76cr.

REX FEATURES: 48tr, 50cl, 51bl, 51cr; Sipa Press
48tl, 49tl.

ROBERT HARDING PICTURE LIBRARY: 35tr; K.
Gillham 87bl; Roy Rainford 88tl.

S.M.A.K.: Dirk Pauwels, Ghent 35cl.

STEDELIJKE MUSEA BRUGGE: Groeningemuseum,
The Last Judgement by Hieronymus Bosch 24c, The
Judgement of Cambyses (1498) by Gerard David
24br, The Virgin and Child with Canon van der Paele
by Jan van Eyck 25ca, Secret-Reflet (1902) Fernand
Khnopff 25tr, Portrait of Bruges Family by Jacob van
Oost the Elder 84tl; Memlingmuseum-Sint-
Janshospitaal, St Ursula Shrine by Hans Memling
7ca, 24-25c, The Adoration of the Magi by Hans
Memling 25cr, The Moreel Triptych by Hans
Memling 25bl.

TAVERNE DU PASSAGE: 75tl

TOERISME BRUGGE/BRUGES TOURIST OFFICE:
87cr.

WORLD PICTURES: 62bl; Mike Hughes 56tl; Peter
Scholey 6ca, 8-9c; Louise Thomson 85tr; Oliver
Troisfontaines 86cl.

All other images © Dorling Kindersley. See www.
DKimages.com for more information.

Acknowledgments

Phrase Book: French

In an Emergency

Help!	**Au secours!**	*oh sekoor*
Stop!	**Arrêtez!**	*aret-ay*
Call a doctor	**Appelez un medecin**	*apuh-lay uñ medsañ*
Call the police	**Appelez la police**	*apuh-lay lah pol-ees*
Call the fire brigade	**Appelez les pompiers**	*apuh-lay leh poñ-peeyay*
Where is the nearest telephone?	**Ou est le téléphone le plus proche**	*oo ay luh tehlehfon luh ploo prosh*

Communication Essentials

Yes/No	**Oui/Non**	*wee/noñ*
Please	**S'il vous plaît**	*seel voo play*
Thank you	**Merci**	*mer-see*
Excuse me	**Excusez-moi**	*exkoo-zay mwah*
Hello	**Bonjour**	*boñzhoor*
Goodbye	**Au revoir**	*oh ruh-vwar*
Good evening	**Bon soir**	*boñ-swar*
morning	**Le matin**	*matañ*
afternoon	**L'apres-midi**	*l'apreh-meedee*
evening	**Le soir**	*swah*
yesterday	**Hier**	*eeyehr*
today	**Aujourd'hui**	*oh-zhoor-dwee*
tomorrow	**Demain**	*duhmañ*
here	**Ici**	*ee-see*
there	**Là bas**	*lah bah*
What?	**Quel/quelle?**	*kel, kel*
When?	**Quand?**	*koñ*
Why?	**Pourquoi?**	*poor-kwah*
Where?	**Où?**	*oo*

Useful Phrases

How are you?	**Comment allez vous?**	*kom-moñ talay voo*
Very well, thank you	**Très bien, merci**	*treh byañ, mer-see*
How do you do?	**Comment ça va?**	*kom-moñ sah vah*
See you soon	**A bientôt**	*ah byañ-toh*
That's fine	**Ça va bien**	*sah vah byañ*
Where is/are ...?	**Où est/sont ...?**	*ooh ay/soñ*
Which way to ...?	**Quelle est la direction pour ...?**	*kel ay lah deer-ek-syoñ poor*
Do you speak English?	**Parlez-vous Anglais?**	*par-lay voo oñg-lay?*
I don't understand	**Je ne comprends pas**	*zhuh nuh kom-proñ pah*
I'm sorry	**Excusez-moi**	*exkoo-zay mwah*

Shopping

How much?	**C'est combien?**	*say kom-byañ*
I would like ...	**Je voudrais**	*zhuh voo-dray*
Do you have ...?	**Est-ce que vous avez ...?**	*es-kuh voo zavay*
Do you take credit cards?	**Est-ce que vous acceptez les cartes de crédit?**	*es-kuh voo zaksept-ay leh kart duh kreh-dee*
What time do you open/close?	**A quelle heure vous êtes ouvert/ fermé?**	*ah kel urr voo zet oo-ver/ fermay*
this one	**celui-ci**	*suhl-wee see*
that one	**celui-là**	*suhl-wee lah*
expensive	**cher**	*shehr*
cheap	**pas cher, bon marché**	*pah shehr, boñ mar-shay*

size (clothing)	**la taille**	*tye*
white	**blanc**	*bloñ*
black	**noir**	*nwahr*
red	**rouge**	*roozh*
yellow	**jaune**	*zhownh*
green	**vert**	*vehr*
blue	**bleu**	*bluh*

Types of Shop

bakery	**la boulangerie**	*booloñ-zhure*
bank	**la banque**	*boñk*
bookshop	**la librairie**	*lee-brehree*
butcher	**la boucherie**	*boo-shehree*
cake shop	**la pâtisserie**	*patee-sree*
chemist	**la pharmacie**	*farmah-see*
chip shop/stand	**la friterie**	*free-tuh-ree*
chocolate shop	**le chocolatier**	*shok-oh-lah-tyeh*
delicatessen	**la charcuterie**	*shah-koo-tuh-...*
department store	**le grand magasin**	*groñ maga-ze*
fishmonger	**la poissonerie**	*pwasson-ree*
greengrocer	**le marchand de légumes**	*mar-shoñ du lay-goom*
hairdresser	**le coiffeur**	*kwafuhr*
market	**le marché**	*marsh ay*
newsagent	**le magasin de journaux/tabac**	*maga-zañ du zhoor-no/ta-b*
post office	**le bureau de poste**	*boo-roh duh pohst pos-tah-leh*
shop	**le magasin**	*maga-zañ*
supermarket	**le supermarché**	*soo-pehr-marshay*
travel agency	**l'agence de voyage**	*azhons duh vwayazh*

Sightseeing

art gallery	**la galérie d'art**	*galer-ree dart*
bus station	**la gare routière**	*gahr roo-tee-yehr*
cathedral	**la cathédrale**	*katay-dral*
church	**l'église**	*aygleez*
closed on public holiday	**fermeture jour ferié**	*fehrmeh-tur zhoor fehree-d*
garden	**le jardin**	*zhah-dañ*
library	**la bibliothèque**	*beebleeo-tek*
museum	**le musée**	*moo-zay*
railway station	**la gare (SNCF)**	*gahr (es-en-say-ef)*
tourist office	**les informations**	*uñ-for-mah-syoñ*
town hall	**l'hôtel de ville**	*ohtel duh vil*
train	**le train**	*trañ*

Staying in a Hotel

Do you have a vacant room?	**est-ce que vous avez une chambre?**	*es-kuh voo zavay oon shambr*
double room	**la chambre à deux personnes**	*shambr ah duh per-son*
with double bed	**avec un grand lit**	*ah-vek uñ groñ lee*
twin room	**la chambre à deux lits**	*shambr ah duhlee*
single room	**la chambre à une personne**	*shambr ah oon pehr-son*
room with a bath	**la chambre avec salle de bain**	*shambr ah-vek sal duh bañ*
shower	**une douche**	*doosh*
I have a reservation	**J'ai fait une reservation**	*zhay fay oon ray-zehrva-syoñ*

40

ing Out

you got a ?	**Avez vous une table libre?**	*avay-voo oon tahbl leebr*
uld like to	**Je voudrais**	*zhuh voo-dray*
rve	**réserver**	*rayzehr-vay*
ble	**une table**	*oon tahbl*
bill, please	**L'addition, s'il vous plait**	*l'adee-syoñ, seel voo play*
a	**Je suis**	*zhuh swee*
arian	**végétarien**	*vezhay-tehryañ*
ress	**Garçon/ Mademoiselle**	*gahso-hn/ mad-uh-mwah-zel*
u	**le menu**	*men-oo*
list	**la carte des vins**	*lah kart-deh vañ*
e	**verre**	*vehr*
	la bouteille	*boo-tay*
	le couteau	*koo-toh*
	la fourchette	*for-shet*
	la cuillère	*kwee-yehr*
kfast	**le petit déjeuner**	*puh-tee day-zhuh-nay*
	le déjeuner	*day-zhuh-nay*
er	**le dîner**	*dee-nay*
course	**le grand plat**	*groñ plah*
	l'hors d'oeuvres	*or duhvr*
ert	**le dessert**	*duh-zehrt*
of the day	**le plat du jour**	*plah doo joor*
	le bar	*bah*
	le café	*ka-fay*
um	**saignant**	*say-nyoñ*
	à point	*ah pwañ*
done	**bien cuit**	*byañ kwee*

nu Decoder

eau	*ahyoh*	lamb
	eye	garlic
erges	*ahs-pehrj*	asparagus
loup	*bah/loo*	bass
mer	*duh mare*	
uf	*buhf*	beef
het	*brosh-ay*	pike
	kah-fay	coffee
au lait	*kah-fay oh lay*	white coffee
e latte	*kah-fay lat-uh*	milky coffee
ard	*kanar*	duck
/chevreuil	*surf/shev-roy*	venison
on	*shee-koñ*	Belgian endive
colat chaud	*shok-oh-lah shoh*	hot chocolate
ux de	*shoo duh*	Brussels sprouts
xelles	*broocksell*	
uille	*kok-eel sañ jak*	scallop
nt-Jacques		
e	*crayp*	pancake
ette	*kreh-vet*	prawn
ade	*doh-rad*	sea bream
ard	*aypeenar*	spinach
ant	*feh-zoñ*	pheasant
s	*freet*	chips/fries
s	*frwee*	fruit
ffre	*gohfr*	waffle
ng	*ah-roñ*	herring
cots	*arrykoh*	haricot beans
cots verts	*arrykoh vehr*	green beans
ard	*oh-ma*	lobster
re	*weetr*	oyster
d'orange	*zhoo doh-ronj*	orange juice
u	*oh*	water
n	*vañ*	wine
mes	*lay-goom*	vegetables
nade	*lee-moh-nad*	lemonade

lotte	*lot*	monkfish
moule	*mool*	mussel
poisson	*pwah-ssoñ*	fish
pommes de terre	*pom-duh tehr*	potatoes
porc	*por*	pork
poulet	*poo-lay*	chicken
raie	*ray*	skate
saumon	*soh-moñ*	salmon
thé	*tay*	tea
thon	*toñ*	tuna
truffe	*troof*	truffle
truite	*trweet*	trout
une bière	*byahr*	beer
veau	*voh*	veal
viande	*vee-yand*	meat
vin maison	*vañ may-sañ*	house wine

Numbers

0	**zéro**	*zeh-roh*
1	**un**	*uñ, oon*
2	**deux**	*duh*
3	**trois**	*trwah*
4	**quatre**	*katr*
5	**cinq**	*sañk*
6	**six**	*sees*
7	**sept**	*set*
8	**huit**	*weet*
9	**neuf**	*nerf*
10	**dix**	*dees*
11	**onze**	*oñz*
12	**douze**	*dooz*
13	**treize**	*trehz*
14	**quatorze**	*katorz*
15	**quinze**	*kañz*
16	**seize**	*sehz*
17	**dix-sept**	*dees-set*
18	**dix-huit**	*dees-zweet*
19	**dix-neuf**	*dees-znerf*
20	**vingt**	*vañ*
21	**vingt-et-un**	*vañ ay uhn*
30	**trente**	*tront*
40	**quarante**	*karoñt*
50	**cinquante**	*sañkoñt*
60	**soixante**	*swahsoñt*
70	**septante**	*setoñt*
80	**quatre-vingt**	*katr-vañ*
90	**quatre-vingt-dix/ nonante**	*katr vañ dees/ nonañt*
100	**cent**	*soñ*
1000	**mille**	*meel*
1,000,000	**million**	*miyoñ*

Time

What is the time?	**Quelle heure?**	*kel uhr*
one minute	**une minute**	*oon mee-noot*
one hour	**une heure**	*oon uhr*
half an hour	**une demi-heure**	*oon duh-mee uhr*
half past one	**une heure et demi**	*uhr ay duh-mee*
a day	**un jour**	*zhuhr*
a week	**une semaine**	*suh-mehn*
a month	**un mois**	*mwah*
a year	**une année**	*annay*
Monday	**lundi**	*luñ-dee*
Tuesday	**mardi**	*mah-dee*
Wednesday	**mercredi**	*mehrkruh-dee*
Thursday	**jeudi**	*zhuh-dee*
Friday	**vendredi**	*voñdruh-dee*
Saturday	**samedi**	*sam-dee*
Sunday	**dimanche**	*dee-moñsh*

Phrase Book: Dutch

In an Emergency

Help!	**Help!**	help
Stop!	**Stop!**	stop
Call a doctor!	**Haal een dokter!**	Haal uhndok-tur
Call the police!	**Roep de politie!**	Roop duh poe-leet-see
Call the fire brigade!	**Roep de brandweer!**	Roop duh brahnt-vheer
Where is the nearest telephone?	**Waar is de dichtsbijzijnde telefoon?**	Vhaar iss duh dikst-baiy-zaiyn duh tay-luh-foan
Where is the nearest hospital?	**Waar ist het dichtsbijzijnde ziekenhuis**	Vhaar iss het dikst-baiy-zaiyn -duh zee-kuh-hows

Communication Essentials

Yes	**Ja**	yaa
No	**Nee**	nay
Please	**Alstublieft**	ahls-tew-bleeft
Thank you	**Dank u**	dhank-ew
Excuse me	**Pardon**	pahr-don
Hello	**Hallo**	haa-lo
Goodbye	**Dag**	dahgh
Good night	**Goedenacht**	ghoot-e-naakt
morning	**Morgen**	mor-ghugh
afternoon	**Middag**	mid-dahgh
evening	**Avond**	av-vohnd
yesterday	**Gisteren**	ghis-tern
today	**Vandaag**	van-daagh
tomorrow	**Morgen**	mor-ghugh
here	**Hier**	heer
there	**Daar**	daar
What?	**Wat?**	vhat
When?	**Wanneer?**	vhan-eer
Why?	**Waarom?**	vhaar-om
Where?	**Waar?**	vhaar
How?	**Hoe?**	hoo

Useful Phrases

How are you?	**Hoe gaat het ermee?**	Hoo ghaat het er-may
Very well, thank you	**Heel goed, dank u**	Hayl ghoot, dhank ew
How do you do?	**Hoe maakt u het?**	Hoo maakt ew het
See you soon	**Tot ziens**	Tot zeens
That's fine	**Prima**	Pree-mah
Where is/are ...?	**Waar is/zijn ...?**	vhaar iss/zayn
How far is it to ...?	**Hoe ver is het naar ...?**	Hoo vehr iss het nar
How do I get to ...?	**Hoe kom ik naar ...?**	Hoo kom ik nar
Do you speak English?	**Spreekt u engels?**	Spraykt uw eng-uhls
I don't understand	**Ik snap het niet**	Ik snahp het neet
Could you speak slowly?	**Kunt u langzamer praten?**	Kuhnt ew lahng-zarmer-praat-tuh
I'm sorry	**Sorry**	sorry

Shopping

I'm just looking	**Ik kijk alleen even**	ik kaiyk alleyn ay-vuh
How much does this cost?	**Hoeveel kost dit?**	hoo-vayl kost dit
What time do you open?	**Hoe laat gaat u open?**	hoo laat ghaat ew opuh
What time do you close?	**Hoe laat gaat u dicht?**	hoo laat ghaat ew dikht
I would like ...	**Ik wil graag ...**	ik vhil ghraakh

Do you have ...?	**Heeft u ...?**	hayft ew
Do you take credit cards?	**Neemt u credit cards aan?**	naymt ew c cards aan
Do you take travellers' cheques?	**Neemt u reischeques aan?**	naymt ew raiys-sheks
This one	**Deze**	day-zuh
That one	**Die**	dee
expensive	**duur**	dewr
cheap	**goedkoop**	ghoot-koap
size	**maat**	maat
white	**wit**	vhit
black	**zwart**	zvhahrt
red	**rood**	roat
yellow	**geel**	ghayl
green	**groen**	ghroon
blue	**blauw**	blah-ew

Types of Shop

antique shop	**antiekwinkel**	ahn-teek-vh kul
bakery	**bakkerij**	bah-ker-aiy
bank	**bank**	bahnk
bookshop	**boekwinkel**	book-vhin-ku
butcher	**slagerij**	slaakh-er-aiy
cake shop	**banketbakkerij**	bahnk-et-bai er-aiy
chip stop/stand	**patatzaak**	pah-taht-zak
chemist/ drugstore	**apotheek**	ah-poe-taiyk
delicatessen	**delicatessen**	daylee-kah-suh
department store	**warenhuis**	vhaah-uh-houws
fishmonger	**viswinkel**	viss-vhin-kul
greengrocer	**groenteboer**	ghroon-tuh-
hairdresser	**kapper**	kah-per
market	**markt**	mahrkt
newsagent	**krantenwinkel**	krahn-tuh-vl kul
post office	**postkantoor**	pohst-kahn-i
supermarket	**supermarkt**	sew-per-ma
tobacconist	**sigarenwinkel**	see-ghaa-ru vhin-kul
travel agent	**reisburo**	raiys-bew-ro

Sightseeing

art gallery	**gallerie**	ghaller-ee
bus station	**busstation**	buhs-stah-shown
bus ticket	**kaartje**	kaar-tyuh
cathedral	**kathedraal**	kah-tuh-drac
church	**kerk**	kehrk
closed on public holidays	**op feestdagen gesloten**	op fayst-dac ghuh ghuh-slow-
day return	**dagretour**	dahgh-ruh-t
garden	**tuin**	touwn
library	**bibliotheek**	bee-bee-yo-
museum	**museum**	mew-zay-uni
railway station	**station**	stah-shown
return ticket	**retourtje**	ruh-tour-tyul
single journey	**enkeltje**	eng-kuhl-tyu
tourist information	**dienst voor toerisme**	deenst vor tor-ism
town hall	**stadhuis**	staht-houws
train	**trein**	traiyn

Staying in a Hotel

double room with double bed	**een twees persoons- kamer met een twee persoonsbed**	uhn tvhays per-soans- ka-mer met vhay per-soans b

room	eenpersoons-kamer	ayn-per-soans kaa-mer
room	een kamer	uhn kaa-mer
	met een lits-jumeaux	met uhn lee-zjoo-moh
with a /shower	kaamer met bad/ douche	kaa-mer met baht/doosh
ou have a nt room?	Zijn er nog kamers vrij?	zaiyn er nokh kaa-mers vray
e a vation	Ik heb gereserveerd	ik hehp ghuh-ray-sehr-veert

ng Out

you got le?	Is er een tafel vrij?	iss ehr uhn tah-fuhl vraiy
ld like to ve a table	Ik wil een tafel reserveren	ik vhil uhn tah-fel ray-sehr-veer-uh
ill, please	Mag ik afrekenen	muhk ik ahf-ray-kuh-nuh
a vegetarian	Ik ben vegetariër	ik ben fay-ghuh-taah-ree-er
ss/waiter	serveerster/ober	sehr-veer-ster/oh-ber
	de kaart	duh kaahrt
list	de wijnkaart	duh vhaiyn-kart
	het glass	het ghlahss
	de fles	duh fless
	het mes	het mess
	de vork	duh fork
	de lepel	duh lay-pul
fast	het ontbijt	het ont-baiyt
	de lunch	duh lernsh
r	het diner	het dee-nay
course	het hoofdgerecht	het hoaft-ghuh-rekht
ir, course	het voorgerecht	het vhor-ghuh-rekht
rt	het nagerecht	het naa-ghuh-rekht
of the day	het dagmenu	het dahg-munh-ew
	het cafe	het kaa-fay
	het eetcafe	het ayt-kaa-fay
	rare	"rare"
um	medium	"medium"
lone	doorbakken	door-bah-kuh

u Decoder

appels	aard-uppuhls	potatoes
rges	as-puhj	asparagus
	beeh	beer
ola	sho-koh-laa	hot chocolate
	aynt	duck
nt	fay-zanh	pheasant
	foh-ruhl	trout
es	free-tyuhs	Chips/fries
vruchten	vroot/vrooh-tuh	fruit
aal	gar-nall	prawn
nten	ghroon-tuh	vegetables
g	haa-ring	herring
vlees	karfs-flayss	veal
	kip	chicken
ook	knoff-loak	garlic
e	koffee	coffee
t	krayft	lobster
vlees	lahms-flayss	lamb
zeeduivel	lot/seafuhdul	monkfish
raalwater	meener-aahl-vhaater	mineral water
el	moss-uhl	mussel
er	ouhs-tuh	oyster
ekoek	pah-nuh-kook	pancake
	snoek	snook

princesbonen	prins-ess-buh-nun	green beans
ree (bok)	ray	venison
rog	rog	skate
rundvlees	ruhnt-flayss	beef
Sint	sind-	scallop
Jacoboester/ Jacobsschelp	yakob-ouhs-tuh/ yakob-scuhlp	
snijbonen	snee-buh-nun	haricot beans
spinazie	spin-a-jee	spinach
spruitjes	spruhr-tyuhs	Brussels sprouts
thee	tay	tea
tonijn	tuhn-een	tuna
truffel	truh-fuhl	truffle
varkensvlees	vahr-kuhns-flayss	pork
verse jus	vehr-suh zjhew	fresh orange juice
vis	fiss	Fish
vlees	flayss	meat
wafel	vaff-uhl	waffle
water	vhaa-ter	water
wijn	vhaiyn	wine
witloof	vit-lurf	Belgian endive/chicory
zalm	sahlm	salmon
zeebars	see-buhr	bass
zeebrasem	zee-brah-sum	sea bream

Numbers

1	een	ayn
2	twee	tvhay
3	drie	dree
4	vier	feer
5	vijf	faiyf
6	zes	zess
7	zeven	zay-vuh
8	acht	ahkht
9	negen	nay-guh
10	tien	teen
11	elf	elf
12	twaalf	tvhaalf
13	dertien	dehr-teen
14	veertien	feer-teen
15	vijftien	faiyf-teen
16	zestien	zess-teen
17	zeventien	zayvuh-teen
18	achtien	ahkh-teen
19	negentien	nay-ghuh-tien
20	twintig	tvhin-tukh
21	eenentwintig	aynuh-tvhin-tukh
30	dertig	dehr-tukh
40	veertig	feer-tukh
50	vijftig	faiyf-tukh
60	zestig	zess-tukh
70	zeventig	zay-vuh-tukh
80	tachtig	tahkh-tukh
90	negentig	nayguh-tukh
100	honderd	hohn-durt
1000	duizend	douw-zuhnt
1,000,000	miljoen	mill-yoon

Time

One minute	een minuut	uhn meen-ewt
one hour	een uur	uhn ewr
half an hour	een half uur	een hahlf uhr
half past one	half twee	hahlf twee
a day	een dag	uhn dahgh
a week	een week	uhn vhayk
a month	een maand	uhn maant
a year	een jaar	uhn jaar
Monday	maandag	maan-dahgh
Tuesday	dinsdag	dins-dahgh
Wednesday	woensdag	vhoons-dahgh
Thursday	donderdag	donder-dahgh
Friday	vrijdag	vraiy-dahgh
Saturday	zaterdag	zaater-dahgh
Sunday	zondag	zon-dahgh

Brussels: Selected Street Index